SOUTHERN JUSTICE: BROKEN IN EVERY WAY

A ROAD TO NO END

by Governor Henderson Jr.

Stella Nova Publishing

Rose Hill, KS

Henderson/Stella Nova Publishing

PO Box 220

Rose Hill, KS/67133

www.stellanovapublishing.com

Book Layout ©2017 BookDesignTemplates.com

Disclaimer: This book reflects the author's present recollections of various people and experiences over time. Names, locations, and identifying details have been changed, some events have been compressed, and some dialogue has been recreated in order to respect and protect the privacy of the individuals involved. Any resemblance to actual persons, living or dead, or actual events, is purely coincidental.

Southern Justice: Broken in Every Way/ Governor Henderson Jr. —1st ed.

ISBN Paperback: 978-1-954077-00-3

Ebook: 978-1-954077-01-0

Many trailblazers and pioneers have contributed to my passion to compose this book, such as Dr. Martin Luther King Jr., Congressman John Lewis, Harriett Tubman, and many others.

However, I dedicate this book to my wife Anthia, who always encourages and motivates me to be steadfast, never wavering, and committed to justice.

I extend this dedication to my mother and father, Carrie Henderson and the late Governor Henderson Sr. Both taught me that integrity and character have no boundaries and to forever stand for those things you believe in.

Contents

We cannot embrace patriotism until we welcome equality, fairness, and justice.

—Governor Henderson Jr.

PREFACE

The core and foundation of authority for our American justice system formed in the 1800s, after the Revolutionary War. In the 1600s and 1700s, night watchmen, volunteers, and appointed sheriffs were used to maintain order. Complaints of unsatisfactory performance included such things as sleeping or drinking while working assignments. The increase in population paved the way for the formation of a major police department. Boston's department formed first, in 1838, followed by New York, Chicago, Philadelphia, New Jersey, New Orleans, and Baltimore. By the 1880s, all major cities had established a police force (plsonline.eku.edu). However, it was our United States Constitution, in 1787, that gave true power and authority to an established government to govern our American justice system. The constitution was ratified in 1788 in order to loosen the reins which were given to the government through the original constitution (history.com). The cloth of our justice system has woven a winding path derived from common law, also known as "judicial precedent." This can be better understood as "judge-made law," or in our current perspective, "case law." Collecting or observing past legal incidents and decisions is a practice that allows case law to be an accepted and otherwise fair practice, even today.

Henry Blaze Wisper, whose experiences are laid out in this book, closely observed the words of our constitution: "We, the people of the United States, in order to form a more perfect union..." Although it may never be achieved in reality, "we the people" have forever chased this dream. "We the people" have continuously faced discrimination, disparities in just punishment, and excessive force by government institutions, whose members swear and participate in solemn oaths aimed at providing liberty and justice for all. Because we can't change history, we can only tell the story and push forward to change any negatives that define our present and future state. This mission is exactly what Henry set out to do. He took his discipline and courage and used it as a foundation to protect others and bring change by serving as a criminal justice professional. The plateau of his career would also be the engine that drove his passion for change.

Henry's career in the criminal justice system began with his work as a prison correctional officer. He wanted to see how the criminal justice system operated by seeing the worst outcome that any person would face if they fell prey to its system. After spending years walking gloomy and dismal prison hallways and monitoring inmates, he'd seen enough. Henry took this foundation and furthered his opportunity to impact crime and provide justice by becoming a police officer in the Southeast region of the United States. His career took off, and he spent the next seven years learning the role of police officer and advancing as one of the best investigators to drive the streets of America. His training gave him a wealth of knowledge in fighting crime, such as drug investigation, burglary, fraud, and theft. Throughout his training, Henry never stopped looking for ways to help those who were most impacted by the justice system. This is why, in order to help victims heal, he transitioned his entire career into enforcing law and investigating crime as a criminal investigator in a prosecutor's office. The first day he walked through the building where he'd set out to change lives, he read signs posted on the walls that said, "It is the policy of this county's district attorney's office that there will be equal opportunity for every citizen, employee, and applicant based upon merit without regard to race, color, religion, national origin, gender, age, genetics, disability, or sexual orientation." These words, while stated clearly, were not always followed. However, Henry planned to do everything in his power to make these words a reality by resisting any and all corruptible acts which did otherwise.

Merriam-Webster online defines corruption as:

a: impairment of integrity, virtue, or moral principle: depravity

b: decay, decomposition

c: inducement to wrong by improper or unlawful means (as bribery)

d: a departure from the original or from what is pure or correct.

As anyone can see, corruption poses potential problems for society and, if not addressed, places the values they hold true at great risk. Such corruption speaks to the need of urgent justice reform. Henry's efforts to maneuver through a damaged justice system is a reflection of its rich history of refusing to change—it is a system that chooses who it serves as well as how it serves.

Our justice system hangs onto its foundational beliefs, those that form a long-lasting record of disparities, not only in justice, but also in the way they navigate the necessities of life—including employment—and the ways they view and treat one another.

Henry's passion to fight for victims of crime was no coincidence. His last position as a police investigator gave him the experience to work in the special victim's division for a large police agency in the Southeast region of the country. The primary focus was to investigate crimes against women and children. After gaining experience, Henry thought that if he could assist with investigating the crimes, he could better serve victims by assisting in the prosecution by bringing the responsible persons to justice. This drove his decision to transition to prosecuting investigator.

An investigator position in any district attorney's office can be powerful, influential, and important because it assists with prosecuting cases where victims have been violated by offenders accused of felony crimes. These crimes include but are not limited to robbery, sexual abuse, rape, and murder. Part of Henry's duties involved locating victims and witnesses who might be difficult to reach or who were simply refusing to cooperate with the criminal justice process. Other responsibilities involve making contact with individuals to serve them with subpoenas to attend court. Many of the individuals encountered had lost confidence and trust in a justice system had been anything but fair and supportive, by maintaining a variety of juggernauts over their lives and the communities in which they lived.

Henry's position was critical, as it included investigations and the case preparation of victims involving sexual assault and crimes against women and children. These investigations are also associated with drug trade, gang violence, and initiations, along with large-scale prostitution and human trafficking. These duties and responsibilities were not intimidating to Henry, because he had a strong work ethic and a drive for success. His accomplishments included the highest academic achievement in his police academy, several awards for police officer of the month, investigator of the year, meritorious service award, and letters of commendation and appreciation. He also received a letter of acknowledgment and recognition from a former governor while working an Olympic Games ceremony.

Henry had a progressive path to success, with an exemplary platform which he filled by being an ethical and determined professional.

ACKNOWLEDGMENTS

I hereby acknowledge the following people and organizations for their contributions to this book. My supportive wife and best friend, Anthia Henderson, and my son Jaylen Henderson, both of whom inspired me to stay focused and grounded during this process. To my diligent and outstanding editor and project manager Diana Grabau, of Stella Nova Publishing.

But most of all, I acknowledge the civil rights movement and its pioneers, who have afforded us the ability and courage to fight for equality, fairness, and justice.

INTRODUCTION

When the framers of our constitution composed the judiciary bodies, the Supreme Court implemented prosecutorial authority, which included immunity for acts committed by both federal and lower courts. Even though acts and decisions may have violated the rights of defendants, no liability would occur, so long as the actions did not violate clearly established criminal or constitutional laws. Simply put, immunity protects from civil liabilities, even when rules are broken. Even rule violations, such as accepting pleas, could impact a criminal case and be grounds for appeal. The rules and accepted practices may vary, depending upon the courts and jurisdiction.

Yes, there are rules, but they sway the pendulum from merely breaking rules all the way to violating constitutional rights to a fair trial. Because the laws are loosely defined, immunity serves as the savior for those in law enforcement who violate justice. In other words, if we can say or show that the intentions were good, anything we do as the government must be given a pass (www.acslaw.org).

Even though immunity makes no mention of negligence, Merriam-Webster online defines "negligence" as "a failure to exercise the care that a prudent person usually exercises" in those circumstances. Although negligence is not a law violation or defined rule, it does by definition define care, and should be considered when seeking justice.

It appears the constitution protects the justice system but does not prioritize the protection of citizens. The ratification of the constitution established guidelines to ensure that the government would not interfere with the fundamental rights of the people, such as due process. But this due process, which must respect all legal rights owed a person, still evades the less fortunate. The balances of power which dictate the laws of the land have been overpowered by governmental control, making constitutional rights obsolete, or in a sense, only imaginary. In order to overcome this illusion, they must restore a balance that was once defined in the constitution by demanding a judicial system of transparency and accountability that establishes trust.

Today, we see a justice system that has failed on many occasions to show fairness and equality. Justice and law enforcement officials who have taken oaths to uphold justice have manipulated society and been protected while doing so. Justice has no limits; rather, its civil or criminal nature and its ability to seek the truth should always be first and foremost. A prosecutor and the prosecuting office within the justice system controls every aspect of how justice is applied or freedom restored. However, when there is abuse of power—fear— there is never justice.

Although police across the world have faced much scrutiny, the future of all aspects of our justice system across the globe rest with those who prosecute and their entities. When prosecutors and law enforcement members fail to meet and understand the needs of society in any manner or relate to generational changes, their actions in administering justice are subject to bias and discriminatory and prejudiced beliefs. These beliefs ultimately display disparities in any form of justice as well as revealing unfair treatment. Based upon the Civil Rights Act of 1871, under 42 U.S.C. § 1983, the command that "every person" who, acting under color of law, violates the rights of another, "shall be liable to the party injured." However, when acts or violations take place at the hands of prosecutors or their entities, a demand for accountability for criminal acts is almost nonexistent. This exemption sends a message that there are no criminal liabilities for intentional or unintentional legal misconduct and establishes a culture that has to win at any cost, with no repercussion. This demeanor throughout history has punished the innocent and failed to provide justice to victims and members of society.

Henry gave of himself in the fight for justice by not only serving as a law enforcing criminal justice professional, but also by wanting to build a foundation to raise awareness of ethical and transparent justice to all of society. Henry's career as a prosecuting investigator will take us on a journey through the pages of this book and will not only express the need for justice reform, but also return us to the values that the constitution was orchestrated to give, those that we believe are equality and justice. While so many looked to understand what justice was, Henry simply wanted to serve and promote fairness. His journey began just before the fall of 2013. His challenges were designed to raise awareness that the same entity that swears to serve, protect, and fight for quality of life has not held true to those standards.

Henry has always had a willingness to promote fairness and believes that opportunities should be offered to all but presented to only the most qualified. One of his areas of concern, and today's struggle in society, is discrimination. This not only affects the way we earn a living, but the way we are viewed and accepted as individuals. Discrimination in the workplace determines who is hired, promoted, or terminated. Even those with the best talent may avoid addressing discriminatory issues, when observed, and to transition elsewhere rather than to challenge the issues.

A district attorney's office is the last stop for victims in the process of receiving justice, and it is tasked with prosecuting those responsible for crimes. This responsibility should be championed and deserves to be treated with the utmost care. Achieving this task takes a combination of commitment and dedication from both management and employees. These are the ones responsible for carrying out the system's goals. The first step should be to hire and retain qualified staff, from management to the front lines, to achieve success.

Criminal investigators and attorneys are ultimately responsible for establishing the elements needed to reach a successful outcome of the criminal trial process. Investigators locate and subpoena witnesses and victims needed for court testimony and also pursue and obtain legal evidence to support criminal prosecution of the case. This position requires the investigator to be familiar with laws regarding prosecution, rules of evidence and presentation, and police practices and operations.

The ability to communicate with and navigate people of diverse backgrounds is a must. If there is a deficiency in any area, it could pose a significant problem when creating a relationship between a prosecuting attorney and an investigator and forming a team atmosphere. The lack of fluency between the two could damage a criminal case, resulting in victims who do not receive the proper justice. Guilty persons can even be set free. Attorneys interpret the law and understanding how it applies to each individual case. However, investigators are the wheels that drive the vehicle, as they have direct contact with the pieces that connect crimes or even dispel them. Investigators handle and pursue criminal evidence, vital witnesses, and observe character and behavioral traits, which are imperative to investigative law.

The background Henry has provided will lend insight into the urgent issues that occur each day around the United States in many district attorney's offices, including Henry's. District attorney agencies often ignore the constant turnover of employees who perform critical tasks by ignoring their needs.

The high turnover results in poor job performance and a lack of quality work, both of which affect the prosecuting of an offense, or the violation of laws through the justice system. It can be easy to identify the troubling issues, but another matter to address and control them.

Some repeat criminal offenders are released from the system because of these issues, forcing their victims to live a life of constant fear. A huge number of backlogged cases take years to reach a resolution. Backlogged criminal cases that have long delays have a direct effect on major stages of the case, such as processing or managing witnesses needed to testify. Witnesses present challenges in these delays, such as changing their testimony from what was previously expected, or suddenly becoming unavailable for trial procedures because they can no longer be located. These incidents by witnesses are not always intentional. Sometimes they've simply forgotten the facts, or they believe the case is no longer a priority of the prosecuting agency. The loss of even one witness, or a change in a previous statement made by a witness, could be the difference between justice for a victim or the release of a potentially guilty offender. The inability to manage witnesses successfully leading up to the actual trial has always been a concern in the criminal justice system. The greatest impact of all this for victims is when they sit in a gloomy courtroom and hear the words "not guilty" read aloud in the verdict.

Many of these negative results are caused by the lack of experienced attorneys assigned to work cases. Some don't have the experience or background in prosecuting specific cases but are selected by their agencies based on the best availability to perform the task rather than on seeking quality results. This effort to inform readers is not intended to exploit the imperfections of any level of government, but to educate and inform while inspiring others to stand up to below-standard procedures and practices. Several events and incidents in this book will deal with public opinion; however, most incidents were those that Henry either witnessed, was a part of, or was made aware of within his criminal justice career. Henry believes we all have a duty to take a close look around us and call out those instances of discrimination, unfair treatment, racism, and intimidation. Take a deep look within and stay determined to make a difference and become the catalyst for change.

Although not all issues require a formal and legal approach, anything worth standing for may very well be worth fighting for. Henry was a simple man who decided that enough was enough. He was willing to sacrifice a career and an upstanding reputation for this very change. He was an individual with love and passion for working in a governmental profession, but he had an even greater passion and commitment to those being served by the government.

As you navigate each passage and paragraph of this book, Henry encourages you to read with focus. Many of the incidents transition from different agencies and departments within the South, but very well may be a different pandemic elsewhere on the planet.

Henry's intentions are to keep readers informed. Many practices and procedures put forth by his district attorney's office seem designed to serve as Band-Aids—to stabilize concerns—until the next set of challenges or a new case presents itself.

Since the Civil Rights Act of 1964, designed to outlaw discriminating work practices based upon race, color, religion, sex, and national origin, there has been continuous verbal progression, but a stalemate in actual progress. Society continues to experience acts of the justice system such as excessive force used by police, favoritism and unfair treatment in the workplace, and the misuse of public funds and taxpayer resources by those who are trusted to manage them.

Politicians, government officials, and attorneys give speeches about zero tolerance for injustice and promotion of change, but very little of that seems to be taking place. Attorneys even advocate to fight for injustices by advertising their experience in growing up within a civil rights movement. Their records highlight only isolated incidents, with no attempt made to voice their current plans or actions to end inequalities.

If justice has not made significant and tangible progress since 1964, what direction is justice headed in addressing positive change? Is there an understanding of the impact of this neglect which strains the public's trust toward the justice system, or of its intentional negligence while accepting bad behavior? Has the government become a revenue-generating business concealed from public view?

Although many sections of the book discuss failed justice practices and concerns, none are intended to advocate for any specific person accused of a crime. However, strenuous efforts to improve practices have failed to give a fair opportunity to employees, citizens, or those accused of a crime. Because the foundation of the book focuses on the practices of a legal environment, all demons should be available for assessment.

Life brings many challenges that force us to contemplate our decisions. The most important ones involve family and the ability to provide and sustain. When issues force us to reconsider our path to financially provide for our families, breadwinners can be forced to operate with many restraints and compromises. Values they should never negotiate include integrity, respect, and fair treatment. Not everyone understands that the denial of these can result in discrimination. The majority of employees who are aware of unfair practices or immoral behavior weigh their choices to either address inequalities or hand over their careers and status, and this dilemma stunts their physical and financial survival.

Often when discrimination or civil rights violations occur, the affected person may be unaware how to address or handle the incident. The indicators of being unlawfully treated are not always obvious and many times are not acknowledged. This forces a person to balance being a victim with sustaining their career, which can be overwhelming. For some, the ability to provide financial support can be the only difference between accepting an unethical or discriminatory demand and refusal to do so, thus standing for truth.

Not all of those accused and later tried for crimes are treated fairly. Victims are routinely treated poorly in the criminal justice system, not only based upon the facts of their cases, but often because they live in areas with lower economic status.

It is impossible to track and determine which deficiencies or acts of negligence that Henry's district attorney's office, or any office, would clean up before publicizing this story. However, everything with processes and information is verifiable to some degree, because all acts have a before-and-after history of changes. When your best defense of the truth is that there is no proof, rather than defending with your own proof, then there is, by general appearance, some concern. Where there is deception there are lies, which hold an internal truth. For those who doubt the relevance of what they have read and witnessed, consider the astonishing turnover numbers in one southern district attorney's office. According to an actual roster Henry was able to view, from the years 2012–2018, the numbers of those who ended their employment in some manner: 38 (2012); 38 (2013); 43 (2014); 55 (2015); 67 (2016); 61 (2017) and 33 (2018). The office employs approximately 100 assistant attorneys and over 100 additional staff members, which include investigators, victim's advocate staff, and administrative personnel.

CHAPTER 1

Who's the Shepherd?

A SHEPHERD IS RESPONSIBLE for making sure that the younger sheep are accounted for and is concerned primarily with their best interests. In the district attorney's office, the chief investigator is the shepherd and is responsible for making sure all investigative procedures are carried out by each of their investigators, who are the sheep.

Although each investigator in the district attorney's office where Henry Wisper served carried out tasks to complete investigations, the responsibility to make sure the work of the investigators met all legal standards of the office and the state rested upon Henry's chief investigator, Dorothy Stoneheart. Before becoming an investigator and then chief investigator, Dorothy's career consisted of working as a police identification technician in the Southeastern region of the United States. Police identification technicians go to crime scenes when called. They photograph the scene and collect any available evidence such as fingerprints, DNA, or blood samples to assist in solving the crime.

Stoneheart worked as a general investigator in the public defender's office and in the prosecutor's office until being appointed chief investigator by the district attorney shortly after he was elected in the late 1990s.

As chief investigator, Stoneheart was responsible for managing every investigator assigned to the DA's office. Stoneheart's important role made her responsible for ensuring every investigator met the state's standards. Investigators processed evidence for trials and managed victims and witnesses needed to prosecute cases.

Stoneheart reported directly to the district attorney, Wilbert Rollins. Rollins too began his career in the '70s as a prosecutor in the solicitor's office, in the Southeast region of the United States. The solicitor is responsible for prosecuting non-felony cases where the accused person could face jail time of up to one year, if found guilty. In the '80s, Rollins's career shifted to the district attorney's office where he served as assistant DA. This office prosecuted felony cases which were assigned to it.

Rollins maintained the position of assistant DA for more than a decade until he ran for the office of district attorney. He was successful in winning the seat.

The primary duties of the DA investigators are to assist attorneys with processing cases for trial by collecting evidence through search warrants and interviewing witnesses and victims, serving subpoenas as needed for future testimony. The case is initiated by police officers or any person who enforces law. Processing felony cases for trial is done by local and county police officers and investigators.

The DA's office job description for the position of investigator included the following duties:

- Conducts investigations and helps assistant DAs prepare cases for trial
- Reviews case files and identifies investigative tasks
- Coordinates investigative plan
- Drafts and executes search warrants or court orders for evidence
- Collects, secures, and analyzes evidence, ensuring chain of custody is maintained

- Assists with interviewing victims and witnesses
- Surveys, photographs, and sketches crime scenes
- Utilizes various investigative tools, resources, and programs to obtain necessary information
- Compiles witness lists
- Consults with assistant district attorneys regarding trial strategies
- Advises grand jury and prosecuting attorneys regarding cases
- Testifies at grand jury or in court.
- Identifies, locates, serves subpoenas, and ensures court appearances of complainants, suspects, victims, and lay and professional witnesses involved in felony cases
- Researches and creates witness files
- Works to obtain full victim/witness cooperation
- Coordinates witness accommodations, such as travel and lodging
- Drafts material witness warrants as needed and coordinates with fugitive units to apprehend witnesses
- Coordinates schedules for court appearances
- Transports and provides security for attorneys, victims, victim advocates, and witnesses
- Escorts attorneys on interviews and crime scene visits
- Provides courtroom security
- Escorts attorneys, victim advocates, and witnesses to and from trial.
- Provides assistance and advocacy to victims of crimes
- Provides information and updates regarding case status and court proceedings
- Provides resources, referrals, and information to assist victims in recovering from the physical, emotional, and financial impacts of crime (such as counseling, housing, or other social services)

Based upon this vast job description, it would be almost impossible for someone to be successful as an investigator without training and experience.

Of the more than three dozen investigators that were budgeted to work in Henry's DA's office each year, almost everyone would consistently express concern about the way the office was managed by Chief Investigator Stoneheart through conversation to one another. One concern voiced was that the chief, although a certified law enforcement officer, had never served as a police or law enforcement investigator where her duties were to investigate crimes by applying state laws and criminal statutes.

While in his initial job interview at the DA's office, Henry was summoned to step outside the room by Chief Investigator Stoneheart. A few minutes into the interview, Stoneheart had excused herself after a knock on the door. Just down the hall an active trial was in session. Someone who had been part of the ongoing trial in the courtroom was concerned about a possible incident of witness tampering, which is the act of attempting to unlawfully influence or prevent the testimony of a witness during a criminal or civil proceeding. Stoneheart was very much aware of Henry's experience as an investigator. When Stoneheart returned, Henry and the other person in the room looked up, waiting for her to take her seat, but instead, she stood close to the open door and motioned for Henry to step outside the room. With a brisk look on her face she began to question Henry. She asked if a witness could legally be required to speak with investigators in the DA's office. She went on to explain that a current witness was pressured not to show up for trial by a defendant's family member. Henry thought for a moment before responding. He was in disbelief that a seasoned chief investigator was unfamiliar with the general criminal procedures regarding speaking to prospective witnesses. His first thought was that the question was part of the interview process—a test of some kind. However, the more she spoke, the more certain Henry became that she was unaware of what constituted a citizen's right to speak versus what would constitute a pertinent witness scheduled to testify. The failure to take action in speaking with the witness could have led to the witness committing perjury, or it could have compromised the entire case, leaving the victim without justice. It could also result in prosecuting an innocent person. Even though Henry was not hired yet, he was concerned that the lack of leadership from the chief investigator could affect the guidance that was needed to lead the investigators she managed. A good leader should make themselves familiar with primary issues which could arise in their profession, as well as seek the proper training needed to help themselves and others to be successful.

Training courses are available that teach investigators how to conduct interviews and interrogate witnesses who could potentially be one or more of the defendants in a case. This training is entitled "Interviews and Interrogations." However, the more important one is "search and seizure," commonly known as "Fourth Amendment search" in the constitution. This aspect has greater value, as it governs when a person is free to leave, or whether they are compelled to remain and speak to law enforcement officials with the possibility of being detained and arrested.

A good leader does more than make sure those responsible know their jobs; they also ensure the investigators are comfortable *doing* their jobs, and they provide proper resources and direction when needed. This can only be accomplished if leaders are comfortable in the performance of their duties and knowledgeable in the areas needed to guide those they manage.

Once hired as an investigator in the district attorney's office and throughout his career there, Henry observed a constant struggle with *all* investigators experiencing issues over the policy of locating victims and witnesses as opposed to what was expected of them. The policy stated that witnesses and victims who could not be located, or who refused to testify or make themselves available for a subpoena, should be relayed to the prosecuting attorney working that case. The reason for this was so the attorney could process a material witness warrant to be served against the victim or witness.

This process, however, was not consistent when investigators were unsuccessful in locating witnesses and victims to be subpoenaed for trials. When Chief Stoneheart was contacted, she simply advised them to continue the effort while asking other investigators to join them. When Henry and investigators provided names of those witnesses who were not available or could not be located, they were advised by Stoneheart and the attorneys that the DA would not accept their concerns.

Although these concerns appear to be only deviations from policies, the bigger issue was legal. Even if the witnesses and victims were reached, the subpoena process must be provided within the legal timeframes. If the subpoena being served was for a local witness, it required, at a minimum, twenty-four-hour's notice to have the witness appear before the courts. If the witness or victim resided out of state, the process required a "submission of subpoena" request to the judicial circuit in the state where the person resided, and they needed to be served where they resided. The subpoena would then need to be served by law enforcement authorities in that particular state.

These witness subpoena concerns were directly controlled by District Attorney Rollins and Chief Investigator Stoneheart, who were responsible for ensuring that attorneys and investigators were operating with best practices for managing witnesses. Regardless of their best efforts to get the job done, a revolving circle of negative reasons existed as to why the policies and best practices were not adhered to. Those in the circle would always include an investigator, an attorney, the chief investigator, and the district attorney. No matter how or where the conversation began concerning witnesses and victims, the goal would always be to provide what the district attorney wanted, or to relay the information that the decision made was what he wanted. This leadership and management style created tension among investigators and attorneys, who ultimately should work together to provide resolution to the cases and justice to victims.

If the inconsistencies in handling the cases were known by witnesses and victims, it could directly affect the confidence, or lack of confidence, shown with the case. If the leadership, management, and approach to managing the case had been carried out with confidence, better success with managing, locating, and securing witnesses and victims for sufficient testimony would have been obtained.

Another policy concern was the processing, admission, and retention of evidence. Evidence retention is the responsibility of the investigator, who has to properly store and secure it. However, the chief investigator is responsible for making sure that the policies regarding evidence retention were being adhered to properly. The duties of maintaining an "evidence chain of custody" is perhaps the most important duty of the investigative role. If strict policies and standards are not followed, any case can be compromised, regardless of the evidence.

Stoneheart never demanded or insisted that the security of evidence received by the office be maintained, as it relates to basic criminal procedures and chain of custody guidelines. These guidelines were meant to ensure that a documented record was kept on every source of evidence regarding who came in contact with the evidence and what their purpose was. It also ensured the evidence was secured at all times from unauthorized persons or those without need. This also directly affected the primary rules of evidence, which could be challenged by defense attorneys during any pretrial or proceeding trials. Any evidence which is part of a criminal case must be accounted for, secure, and access allowed only to those with legal need. In addition, the names of those in contact with or involved in the exchange of evidence must be listed within the case documentation.

On a number of occasions, evidence was left in the unsecured offices of investigators before, during, and after trial, directly compromising trial processes. If known, this would ultimately meet the grounds for appeals. An accused person of any crime and the person designated to defend them have the responsibility to ensure that the evidence that might be used against them is truthful, legal, and undisturbed by unauthorized persons.

Henry personally experienced an incident while assisting the homicide unit of the office on a murder case. It was common for investigators to be pulled from their assigned responsibilities to help on other cases, or to have cases assigned to them from other divisions. Henry was directed by his supervisor to take over a case from the assigned investigator. Henry spoke with this investigator, who stated the case was continued at a later date, but she had evidence for it in her office. Henry informed her that she needed to have the evidence properly secured by the evidence custodian, whose responsibility was to secure evidence before trial. This investigator became upset because Henry refused to take the evidence, which should have been taken to a secured location where only authorized staff members could access it. When Henry refused acceptance, she simply left the evidence outside his door, unattended, open to any staff member who walked through the hallway. It was also accessible to the custodial staff responsible for cleaning offices in addition to other civilians who routinely walked through the hallways to be interviewed by other investigators involving other cases.

If the evidence custodian was unavailable, the investigator could have easily returned the evidence to the respective law enforcement agency that originally gathered it until it was needed for trial. Evidence can never be left unattended, and every individual who comes in contact with it must be accounted for.

Even though each investigator had a key to lock their own offices, the keys were all universal, which gave every investigator access to every other investigator's office, as well as to any evidence they were holding. Regardless of the fact all investigators are employees who should be trusted and may work together on cases, the personal contents of their work products should remain exclusive, as it could affect the process of a legal case. If information and contents of cases, such as evidence, are disturbed with no record or documentation, then the legal process is compromised. This leads to bad work practices or unethical misconduct, which unlawfully manipulates the course of justice. Henry made his supervisor aware of the investigator attempting to turn over evidence to him directly rather than taking it to an authorized and secure location until needed for trial. The supervisor of the division contacted him and advised that the evidence had been picked up; however, no details were provided as to who took the evidence nor where it was taken.

Maintaining evidence is a critical part of prosecuting cases in the criminal justice system. It is the responsibility of the chief investigator to implement and enforce a strict policy to properly maintain this evidence. If there are deviations to the policy, clear expectations *must* be provided to those involved in the process of handling evidence.

What's more, approximately three-fourths of the investigators assigned to the DA's office stored evidence in their offices. The chief investigator routinely visited the offices of investigators and had the day-to-day opportunity to address obvious violations of unsecured evidence kept in individual offices.

Another policy concern was the documenting of attendance. Some investigators would simply sign in and out in an attendance book, and attendance would eventually be calculated by the chief investigator. Others were expected to use an electronic swipe card to document attendance. According to a brief, two-paragraph policy, investigators were required to work 8:30 a.m. to 5:00 p.m. and to sign in with his or her assigned supervisor. It specified that whoever was not present for work by 8:45 a.m. would be considered late. There was no mention of which investigators were responsible for using the time-clock system, which is one of the two ways mentioned above for attendance documentation.

Investigators who clocked in after 8:30 a.m. had the minutes they were late deducted from their accumulated paid time off, which reflected on each bi-weekly pay period, and were not allowed to stay late to offset minutes. The inability to clearly document this into a policy allowed a system where investigators who clocked in and out were held to a higher standard of accountability than those who did not use that system. The lack of cohesive policies allowed the chief investigator and the district attorney's office to determine how they wanted to discipline investigators.

Each day Henry struggled to understand how a large organization could employ investigators and attorneys who verbally expressed being uncomfortable in their roles. They would state that their discomfort was caused by a controlling environment, and a lack of consistent standards with policies, both of which were said to be created by District Attorney Wilbert Rollins and Chief Investigator Dorothy Stoneheart.

As the mass of people resigning their positions grew, Henry came to some conclusions. Many employees selected as investigators did not seem to have strong leadership qualities or were unable to make sound decisions for themselves, ultimately allowing an environment of control by the chief investigator. Although Stoneheart conducted the interview process for new hires, each candidate also sat before and spoke to the DA during the process. Even though the primary role of the district attorney was to manage and assist attorneys with the assessment of each case, the chief investigator reported directly to the DA, regardless of her decisions related to the hiring of investigators. This concerned him, as the certification of investigators are managed at the state level.

The chief investigator has a duty to manage and assess investigators based upon their defined qualifications or certifications, not by the desires of the DA, who is a civilian and elected official chosen by taxpayers. If the seasoned and experienced investigators resisted or challenged the control and intimidation efforts of the DA and chief investigator, they would simply be pushed away. Those investigators who did not want to challenge the controlling environment detached themselves or did not associate with the few who attempted to resist the controlling management style.

Many of the investigators who resigned and who spoke to Henry stated that they simply needed peace of mind. This high turnover caused productivity to suffer tremendously. Henry never understood how the county government administration could not identify these concerns within the DA's office unless they knew but feared to address it. If the issues were addressed publicly, the citizens and taxpayers would lose confidence, not only with the county government itself, but also with providing justice to the victims of crimes.

Henry attended an investigator's meeting in December 2016, headed by Stoneheart, which produced new concerns. She informed a few investigators they needed to schedule personal meetings with her.

One of the investigators was very close to Henry, and they shared the experience of being overlooked for promotion. He explained after his meeting that Stoneheart told him it took a while for a promotion, but she was glad he was patient. He was told that three positions for senior investigator were open—major case investigator, gang investigator, and public integrity investigator. Stoneheart instructed him to select one, fill out an application, and his new salary should begin in two weeks. Based upon his conversation with Henry, this meant he was now guaranteed to be promoted without any formal process or announcement, or any attempt by Chief Investigator Stoneheart to seek other investigators who might be interested in open positions.

If the positions were open, the opportunity should be available to every investigator who had the qualifications to do the job. When promotions are given for any position in the county government, Human Resources or personnel departments must also be familiar with the changes that will result in order to compensate for such promotion. When county positions other than investigator or district attorney positions are open, they are accessible through open announcements for all employees, with qualifications highlighted. Henry was aware of this because he applied for two positions himself during his career at the DA's office. District attorney office positions should have been transparent, no different from others.

Even though this investigator was truly overdue for the promotion based upon his hard work, there were still others next in line to be considered for promotion based upon the verbal policy of Stoneheart that she considers seniority and tenure in the DA's office first when considering investigators for promotion.

On several occasions, Stoneheart stated that promotions would be given based upon the combination of meeting work expectations and seniority in the role. The chief investigator's failure to adhere to this practice created day-to-day frustration, which investigators voiced to one another.

In mid-December 2016, while conducting a staff meeting, Stoneheart discussed the upcoming Christmas party scheduled later that evening and mentioned that several people who deserved awards were getting them. She also spoke about the good work of her supervisory staff and each individual effort in the units. This all appeared sincere, until words that were designed to motivate became words which, when compared to actions, were not true.

She added that changes were coming in the future and efforts were being made to promote staff members to senior-level investigators. She said she had promoted one investigator that week after he had been patient and served his time. She finished by saying that regardless of how hard you worked, she did not base promotion upon performance, but entirely on what she phrased as "putting in your time and seniority." The statement "putting in your time" was her personal criteria for promotion, as time is considered seniority based. Stoneheart never clarified what she meant by "putting in your time," and no specified amount of service time, implied or written, had ever been expressed as a requirement in order to be promoted. She also said she had one other promotion to award in the future.

This was deceptive in more ways than one. This same week, Henry spoke to the employee she promoted and was told that Stoneheart had three positions open. However, she claimed she had only one other vacancy. Nobody with seniority was considered for these positions. Henry could personally attest to this, because he had worked in the office for over three years and was not considered for a promotion, nor was he aware of any efforts of the chief investigator or the county to seek investigators for open or vacant positions. Instead, promotional investigator positions were consistently given to those with less seniority.

Even though Henry held a specialized position in the office for two years, he was never advanced to a senior level in that position after he began. According to Stoneheart's verbal policy, investigators who worked in one of the specialized divisions that handle only cases dealing with sexual assaults and homicides were senior investigators upon accepting the role. The senior status itself was identified to be a promotion.

Henry believed this all started and stopped with the chief investigator and the district attorney, both of whom managed every promotional decision within the DA's office. He had always believed that a good leader sets examples and establishes and upholds fair standards. Instead, both the DA and the chief investigator operated with selective standards that were unfair and inconsistent.

In early January 2017, Henry attended a personnel policy and procedure session where the personnel department explained new and revised policies. Attendance and punctuality were the first of the new policies. It was stated there would be possible disciplinary action for employees who took excessive time off work or violated the tardiness policy. The meeting was open to every employee of the county. However, as the administrators discussed the upcoming changes and policies related to attendance, time off work, and disciplinary action, there were differences. They were told these specific policies did not apply to those employed under elected officials, such as the DA's office or the office of the sheriff. This did not sit well with employees who worked in other departments for the county, but no explanation was provided as to why such major policies as attendance and disciplinary action would not apply to every county employee.

Next on the agenda involved equal internal pay. This new set of policies allowed an employee to submit paperwork to have their salary evaluated. If an employee believed their salary was not in line with current or newly hired employees, they could request an assessment, but could only challenge it after being in their position for two years. If the practice was improper, why would an individual need to wait two years for what he or she deserved?

During the session, representatives were asked if physical copies would be available to reference the information in the new policies. They responded that the publication was still in progress, but the changes were effective at the start of 2017.

Many of the employees did not attend the meeting since no mandatory attendance requirement had been given in the meeting notification. It was concerning that there was no way to view the updates or policy changes either online or with a physical copy. Even after Henry attended the meeting in the first week of the new year, he requested a copy of the changes and updates to the policy through the DA's administrative assistant. Employees were told during the policy meetings to address their prospective administrative contact persons for copies of the policy updates. Henry's contact told him that the updates were still not available. This was approximately the third week of the new year of 2017.

Another interesting part of the policy announcements was the one on bullying. Of course, any policy of this type would most likely be "zero tolerance." According to Merriam-Webster online, the definition of a bully is "a person who is threatening, harsh, or cruel to smaller or weaker people," and one could include those who are vulnerable in some way as well. This definition seemed to fit the habitual environment at the district attorney's office to a "T." Stoneheart was comfortable with cursing at and in the presence of investigators, victims, and witnesses on a consistent and habitual basis, and verbally encouraged investigators to be tougher and to call on her when the need arose to be tough with witnesses and victims.

Many investigators, including Henry, saw her in action as she made calls to witnesses and victims. During these conversations she would be rude and profane. This was not his idea of being a tough leader but was instead unprofessional. The bullying policy addressed the work environment related to employees, but this type of behavior and conduct should not be tolerated toward anyone, including the public.

When it comes to management, one must be perfect in only one aspect, and that is customer service. As a manager and leader of any operation, you *are* customer service. You cannot afford to lose one employee or citizen at the hands of substandard service. Although processes and situations may create challenges, the service cannot be compromised.

A leader may spend a lifetime never having the opportunity to supervise others; it is not a requirement. However, a person can never lead until they can be a strong follower. When an individual learns to follow, they become familiar with the challenges a leader may face, therefore understanding the best solutions to address challenges and create a positive environment. Stoneheart always tried to tag herself with a reputation for managing like a mother figure. Neither the investigators nor Henry needed a mother. What they needed was someone to *operate* the office under a set of guidelines and regulations which were fair and consistent. This motherly form of management left the door open to conclude that all policies, rules, and advancements could be selectively enforced.

Many times, when policies were violated by investigators, the only action taken was a harsh scolding of the violator in the weekly staff meetings, sometimes in the presence of everyone. The scolding would consist of greater effort to embarrass the investigator than to correct the behavior with positive reinforcement and an attempt to resolve the issue and prevent future incidents. Most of the comments ended by other investigators laughing, which shifted the goals from teachable moments to merely entertainment. After the chastising was complete, Stoneheart would ask if they would rather be punished or be dealt with like a mother would do. Obviously, no one would choose to be punished.

Just as discipline for policy violations was inconsistent, there was no evaluation process for gauging performance when considering promotions. The process of managing like a mother, in Henry's opinion, gave Stoneheart the ability to be selective with discipline, promotions, and expectations.

The leadership of the office never seemed to improve, and the frustrations compounded when there was no one to turn to about the concerns. The frequent pep talks given by Stoneheart in an effort to bring investigators together as a team resulted only in compensating for those who many times underperformed or were less qualified.

Toward the end of July 2017, which was also the week investigators attended yearly training, Stoneheart sent an email instructing each investigator to make a copy of the training form and the hours that were recorded. The email ended by reminding them that they were law enforcement officers, and that Stoneheart herself attended the training as well. This implied that investigators were not attending the training but were documenting that they had in fact completed the training. Since the training was considered an employee's regular work schedule for that week, this should have carried the same penalty as falsifying work hours, if the behavior was identified in the past. This too was a leadership concern; therefore, the behaviors should have been addressed in previous instances as they were observed. This was not the first time Chief Investigator Stoneheart questioned the integrity and ethics of investigators.

These concerns, like many, showed the lack of implementation or enforcement of specific policy that could discipline performance concerns while upholding integrity. Just as integrity is required in the processing of criminal cases, it should also be required in the day-to-day operations of the justice system. The criminal justice business must continually display the highest character, accountability, and level of transparency which promotes trusted leadership.

In February 2018, early in the new year, new concerns arose about the DA's office. A friend of Henry's from a prior police department was the victim of what he described as disrespect and unprofessional practices displayed by the DA's office. This issue arose from his friend's attempt to take part in the hiring process for an investigator position.

He was scheduled for an interview in January 2018, and upon arrival was told by one of the DA's administrative staff members that his appointment was not for that date and time. He responded that he received notification of the appointment, and he was correct, according to that notification. He was allowed to interview since he was there, but he was placed in line much later, behind other candidates. Once the interview was complete, he received instructions regarding a follow-up, after further review, to see if he was a favorable candidate. He received notice to return for another interview. Upon arrival, he was informed again that he was not expected to be there that day and would be notified what day he should return.

This was strange when compared to Henry's hiring experience. Normally, a second interview would be to confirm one's hiring and to speak with the district attorney. Days passed, and Henry's friend still didn't receive a return call, a follow-up, or a notification. The candidate sent an email to Stoneheart to check on his application status, reporting to Henry that he was professional and to the point in his communication and was trying to be onboard as a team player. Henry asked what happened regarding the confusion with the two previous interview appointments. The friend stated he had been very transparent with everything in his background but had no response to the email. He did receive a call from Stoneheart. She introduced herself, then expressed that she was blown away by the email regarding his experience. Her response, according to him, was that she thought he was trying to manipulate them to get a job there. The email was too long and detailed, she said, adding that she felt he was trying to show that the office was incompetent. In addition, she said the office reserved the right to choose who to interview. This type of response from Stoneheart to a job candidate was concerning. Even though the applicant was attempting to gain employment, he was still a citizen who should have received decent customer service. It appeared she'd already disqualified the candidate as a potential fit for the DA's office.

Although not a requirement, a courteous and respectful action would have been for the office to send some type of notification that another candidate had been selected. He also should have received an apology for the errors that occurred with two incorrect notifications for his appointments. District Attorney Wilbert Rollins and Chief Investigator Dorothy Stoneheart harbored a culture which refused to develop or adhere to standard policies and procedures, and which prevented fair practices to current and future employees.

CHAPTER 2

Meeting the Needs

PEOPLE HIRED AS ATTORNEYS AND INVESTIGATORS are given permission to carry weapons, to touch and encounter drugs, to invade the personal lives of victims, and to influence the fate of defendants.

Investigators routinely discussed concerns regarding other investigators who were hired. Specifically, issues came up with the performance of new hires at their former places of employment. The issues involved whether or not the investigator actually had the experience needed to work in the DA's office. Some investigators knew one another from working together at other law enforcement agencies or knew someone who knew them. Therefore, it was known that some investigators had previous performance or disciplinary issues which would not have made the investigator a good candidate to be hired to work in the office.

Background checks should consist of more than just criminal record and driver's history checks. Verifying a new hire candidate's work history would show all assignments, duties, and responsibilities, including disciplinary actions. Knowing this background is vital to ensure that investigators carrying these heavy burdens of responsibility are not only qualified based on their resumes but are ethically and morally fit to perform their duties.

One investigator, hired from the county's local police agency, was expected to work on DA Rollins's security team. One of the necessary criteria was experience in providing specialized security protection to specific leaders. Later, an investigator familiar with this investigator's experience confirmed to Henry that the investigator had never worked in that capacity and did not have the needed experience. If specific requirements were not met, it was not only the duty of the candidate to be truthful about their experience, but to have the experience confirmed by those hiring. Another concern was the failure of the county and district attorney's offices to conduct drug testing for new hire investigator candidates, who are required to carry firearms. Drug testing is extremely important for anyone who carries a firearm and is authorized to use deadly force. Whether illegal or prescribed, drug use could provide evidence that a person's ability to make good decisions has become compromised. Henry was not familiar with any drug policy established or enforced for investigators by either the district attorney's office or the county. Henry did not undergo a drug test prior to being hired as an investigator and neither did many of the investigators he spoke with.

Investigators were also authorized to operate county-owned vehicles, and some were allowed to drive these vehicles when off duty. Although the county government reserves the right to require and enforce drug testing, citizens should be assured that the decision-making and services provided are not compromised by drug activity.

The failure to establish and enforce a standard drug policy could display to both employees and the public that there is no accountability for drug use or how it could affect work performance. The lack of a standard could also bring transparency into question, because if concerns are uncovered, the issue would have to be addressed and the transgressor punished, causing a lack of public trust and confidence. Imposed punishments would compromise the integrity of the work done with criminal cases, creating a manpower shortage due to disciplinary measures leading to termination.

Efforts to make sure investigators are drug free could also play a major role in processing drug evidence, especially for an office without standards for maintaining the proper chain of custody with evidence. A history existed of employees in the DA's office—including attorneys—who had allegations of reporting to work intoxicated. Surprisingly, this issue did not lead to creating or enforcing a drug policy. All actions of employees, past and present, should be up for assessment.

Chief Investigator Stoneheart struggled at times to communicate to investigators how to carry out specific protocols and legal procedures that DA Rollins wanted done on certain cases, and why they needed doing. She would advise investigators to complete tasks such as search warrants for certain evidence or pursuit of certain witnesses and victims, but when questions arose over the process, or the steps to be taken to legally complete the request, she provided limited or unclear information. She would respond that the request came from the district attorney. This was always a concern, because the certified investigator was responsible for any work completed on cases and was required to provide an explanation of the actions taken. Although the district attorney is the highest authority in the office, the chief investigator is responsible for the actions and decisions of the investigators.

Standards for investigators are governed by the state's certifying council, just as they are for police officers. A traditional law enforcement officer may become the subject of an investigation or be questioned about their duties by their employer. This could lead to disciplinary action by the employer, which could then be passed on and investigated by the state council, who governs the certification of law enforcement personnel. This is why it is imperative that any decision made by law enforcement persons while performing their duties be precise and correct. If the state council investigates a law enforcement office for performance or disciplinary issues passed on by their employer, an officer could lose their certification. Oftentimes investigators in Henry's DA's office were not supervised, especially when guidance was needed. The supervisor, if off work that day, would send an email to other investigators to contact the chief investigator with any concerns or questions, but many times she was not available when called. To compensate, the supervisor would redirect by sending a different email advising all investigators in the division to check with one another or with whoever had a trial to see if they needed assistance. It was not a concern for investigators to assist one another, but without sufficient supervision, no one was available to accept responsibility if actions were later scrutinized.

The DA's office appeared more and more desperate to find qualified investigators. They began hiring people with no investigative background, and many had not worked in a law enforcement position for years. The pickings were extremely slim, and their lack of competence was proven once they began working.

Stoneheart and the supervisors often asked investigators to pitch in and help the inexperienced investigators. Some of the requests included things that should be known by any criminal investigator—basic rules of evidence, how to write and apply for a search warrant, and how evidence should be submitted, maintained, and accepted for trial.

Some didn't know how to obtain a proper DNA sample or how to complete the process once it was collected. Stoneheart did not make consistent efforts to ensure investigators were comfortable performing their duties. She failed to set clear expectations or suggest overall training for investigators in regard to search warrants and evidence processing, both vital to the position.

When Henry observed new investigators attempting to perform their duties, many appeared to not have the foundations to successfully perform their jobs.

The attractive salary brought average law enforcement officers into the DA's office, but no efforts were made to retain experienced or seasoned investigators who were assets to the office. The office's reputation served as only a stop along the way until the investigator figured out where they really wanted to be employed. No taxpayer would be comfortable receiving substandard service, just as no patient would want to undergo surgery with an inexperienced doctor on their first day out of medical school.

Those whose duty it is to safeguard your rights as victims and citizens should be held responsible for your life, just as doctors are. Your path to healing and recovery may very well rest upon an entire team of attorneys and investigators hired not on their qualifications, but only to fill vacant positions. Why the office was no longer able to attract qualified applicants was never explored. Speculation was that former employees were warning off those considering employment. Better the devil you know than the devil you don't. Former employees shared their horror stories, and potential employees were unwilling to take the risk.

It didn't help that the large police departments were familiar with the practices of the DA's office, and the two did not have a respectable relationship. Many law enforcement officers who came to the office to testify would discuss with one another their displeasure with the office. They said the office made them feel incompetent enforcing laws, even though the DA introduced several flaws when prosecuting their cases, including long delays with dispositions and unfamiliarity with cases.

Near the end of 2016 or early 2017, Stoneheart held a staff meeting involving the investigators of Henry's division, during which she discussed expectations and work tasks for the new year. She mentioned that investigators in the unit were expected to meet high demands based upon their qualifications and work experience as sexual assault specialists. She went around the room and pointed out what she knew about each investigator's experience working sexual assault cases based upon their performance with other agencies they worked for, which is why they had been transitioned or hired into the division.

It seemed Stoneheart was not familiar with each investigator's background. Many new hires in the division as well as in the office were moved into special divisions but had never been detectives or investigators.

Investigators who worked together in the office either routinely discussed each other's experience or were familiar with it based on working together, either directly or within the same county or demographics. Many of the new investigators or those with less seniority were assigned to the specialized divisions, such as sexual assault or homicide. Many of the more senior investigators did not desire to go into the specialized divisions because the case work was more complex, the benefits said to come with working the more complex divisions were never consistent, or they simply did not like cases involving sex crimes and murder. Stoneheart's verbal policy was that the specialized positions came with more pay and some with county-assigned vehicles that could be driven home. Most of the investigators working the specialized divisions did not begin receiving their new pay until several months later, if at all, which was the investigators' primary complaint.

As the meeting ended, Stoneheart asked if everyone was fine with doing their jobs and handling their responsibilities. Investigator Litia Sampson was the only investigator who spoke up, saying she was overwhelmed. The chief investigator's face appeared somber and her voice sounded as though the air had left her body. Never at a loss for expressive words, she only said, "Okay, we will discuss it later."

It appeared the chief investigator was not expecting anyone to have concerns in their roles after her earlier statement in the same meeting that investigators were chosen to work the specialized division based upon previous work history and performance. Investigator Sampson, who was hired into the division, did not have previous experience as a detective who investigated crimes or sexual assault investigative experience.

In February 2017, Henry was walking the ever-changing hallways near his office when he observed a new investigator accompanied by a relatively new supervisor. It appeared she was showing him around. Henry was startled at what transpired next. She asked him if it was true that he had been out of law enforcement for the last three years, which he confirmed. Although Henry was not aware of his qualifications and hadn't watched him perform any tasks, it was interesting how someone with a three-year absence from their profession would fare in an environment with the volume of work and responsibilities in the office. Other investigators also mentioned the new investigator's lack of recent experience.

After seeing numerous investigators leave the DA's office, it became clear the office didn't worry about hiring or retaining qualified staff because they did not expect them to stay long. This was the suspicion behind asking new investigators for three-year commitments during the hiring process. It seemed every new investigator was more inexperienced than the last.

During one week in April 2017, Stoneheart gave an assignment to a few investigators, including Henry, to conduct background checks, such as criminal and driving histories, on applicants for office internships. One investigator had no knowledge of how to log into the system to begin performing checks, a basic and vital skill needed for their job. The state required special tracking numbers be obtained for all searches and actions on the checks. When Henry and another investigator inquired about obtaining this number, Stoneheart was hesitant to provide it. She directed them to use their initials and the number seventeen for the year 2017. This number was very important, as it showed the legality for researching sensitive information. Even more important, it protected the employee who connected his or her name to the search process and explained all searches against potential audit.

There appeared to be no clear guidance as to how this process could be conducted successfully and legally. Henry understood the importance of the tracking number, having gone through the process as a police investigator, but the DA's office had different protocols. Being qualified and understanding the responsibility of your role not only helped to produce a high standard of work, it also helped avoid legal and financial challenges. When the state's requirements for conducting searches with the required documentation were violated, it could lead to sanctions and fines against the operator and the agency.

Although any sensitive information search by an investigator is their responsibility, it is also the responsibility of the employer to provide the proper knowledge and education. Are they seeking the best candidates to serve our taxpayers and citizens, or simply offering whatever they can? Are they in search of quality leaders or just those they are more comfortable with?

In spite of all the concerns Henry witnessed in the office, action was never taken by the chief investigator or the district attorney to address the deficiencies that strained the office until they were backed into a corner with their hands tied. Rollins and Stoneheart experienced resistance head on from Henry.

Toward the end of Henry's service in the DA's office, it appeared the office had begun to implement strategies for addressing its deficiencies. In early June 2017, investigators were informed of mandatory training scheduled for the following week. Stoneheart rolled out approximately thirteen areas of responsibility as well as expectations related to the position of investigator. This training had never been mentioned or conducted previously during Henry's career in the district attorney's office.

In June 2017, an attorney in Henry's division said it had become extremely difficult to perform their job responsibilities because the investigators were not doing their jobs. The attorney further explained that the investigator was asking the attorney to write up the facts to be included in the search warrant. Once this was complete, the investigator would take the search warrant to a judge to be reviewed and signed or denied. If signed, the investigator would execute the search warrant to collect evidence for the trial. This was concerning for the attorney, because the attorney has to play a neutral role as it relates to collecting evidence and prosecuting an accused person for that evidence. Normally, investigators and attorneys function as a team, processing the case by reviewing and collecting any further evidence for a trial. The attorney gives the investigator a list of tasks to complete, such as serving subpoenas or requesting evidence. The investigator's responsibility is to be familiar with and understand the elements of a crime along with the rules of evidence, which include the Fourth Amendment to the Constitution—search and seizure—when pursuing evidence which requires a search warrant. The writing of the facts in the search warrant is strictly the duty of investigators or law enforcement officers, who are sworn law enforcement employees. The attorney can assist and guide the investigator with interpreting and understanding the facts included in the search warrant but cannot write the facts for the investigator, and this raised concerns over how often such requests were made of attorneys and the legal conflicts it created. Some lumps under the rug were becoming too big to hide. Even though investigators are assigned to work with one specific attorney, the assignments of investigators and attorneys are sometimes changed. However, the approach and steps the investigator takes toward completing tasks should remain consistent.

If a noncertified law enforcement person writes facts to have a search warrant signed and later provides those facts to the law enforcement person to present as their own findings and facts, the investigator must take a sworn oath before a judge that those facts are true and of their knowledge. These practices could compromise every case an attorney or investigator has ever come in contact with and could also compromise the justice system they represent. The attorney explained that in addition to the legal conflict that could have occurred, there was no confidence in going to the investigator's manager or the manager to whom the attorney reported because neither manager appeared comfortable handling such concerns.

Henry did not receive any update from the attorney on either the approach taken to resolve the concern or the outcome. However, the attorney appeared overwhelmed and stressed and it seemed this situation needed to be addressed.

CHAPTER 3

✻

Mismanagement

MANY INVESTIGATORS WERE HIRED ON at higher and unequal start salaries with no explanation or justification, such as greater experience, education, or a combination of both. Although many investigators may have been unaware, the district attorney's office had a computer database of information available to every investigator.

This information contained forms needed to perform the job in addition to new-hire welcome letters, letters requesting a pay raise, and promotional salary increases. Some of the letters were addressed to the DA by the investigator, while some were written by the DA himself on behalf of investigators and attorneys requesting salary increases.

The requests also displayed salary numbers. Even though some investigators communicated a delay in receiving promotional pay increases, many were required to function under a different level of accountability. Some senior investigators did not have to clock in and reported directly to the chief investigator, though no explanation was given as to why this was so. Some senior investigators were required to clock in like those who were not senior investigators. No overtime was given to those who clocked in, as every investigator was allegedly on a salaried position. Nothing in the job responsibilities defined which investigators were to clock in or why.

The lack of consistency within the DA's office was as confusing as it sounds and reflected the inconsistencies in managing day-to-day operations of the office. Confusion over promotions and salary increases concerned investigators, because it left no system with which to gage performance for advancement or promotion.

The inconsistent process of managing policies and promotions always seemed to be a concern, but the policies appeared to benefit only the leaders in the office. In October 2016, Henry attended a weekly team meeting for his division. The supervisor explained that Chief Investigator Stoneheart would not be retiring as originally planned, which had been discussed in a meeting with investigators weeks prior. However, she would be taking time off in increments of three months, using her accumulated sick time. Even though the chief investigator chastised investigators several times for taking time off when they were not sick, she displayed intentions to do that very thing. According to the county's sick leave policy, approved sick leave requests included incidents involving personal illness, convalescence, nonoccupational injury, exposure to contagious disease, dental or vision treatment, personal emergencies which justify medical leave, or the Family Care Act. The policy also clearly defined that employees would not be compensated for unused sick leave at the end of their employment. However, the policy did not apply to the payout of sick leave to an employee's estate upon the employee's death.

In previous meetings, Stoneheart had accused investigators of abusing sick leave. Nothing was said that led investigators to believe her position and title afforded her the ability to take a large amount of accumulated sick time under any current policy. She would receive pay for such time, whereas those who worked and retired there previously had to forfeit their hours.

Months later, the chief investigator announced during an investigator staff meeting that she had decided not to retire after more than thirty years of service, nor was she taking any time off for personal matters. No one seemed to know why she made a sudden change in her attempt to exhaust her sick time toward retirement as she had announced previously.

The district attorney's office revealed budget issues to employees in 2016. There would be an assessment of furloughs. However, plans to have investigators attend paid conferences for training would not be eliminated, which later created additional financial burdens to the county despite District Attorney Rollins defining the training as mandatory. Once the conference was completed, reimbursements to investigators and attorneys for conference-related expenses were always delayed. This included four-and-a-half hours of one-way travel by vehicle, where fuel, food, and lodging had to be paid upfront. Many investigators who requested financial hardship were denied. A few investigators, including Henry, insisted they could not afford to attend because the county often wouldn't reimburse until months after the training. The chief investigator herself requested the reimbursement on occasion, and she was not bashful in letting everyone know, based upon the roster of those who signed up for the assistance.

Attorneys were required to attend the conference to complete their mandatory training hours for the year, but investigators had other training options that only needed approval from the chief investigator. They could arrange training within the office through investigators who were also certified instructors. This would have allowed training to be received throughout the year as opposed to reimbursing every attorney and investigator within a few months. There were no special incentives given for investigators who were certified instructors, therefore budget issues in that area were not a concern. In November 2016 Henry was speaking with a supervisor while they were waiting on vehicle repairs. The supervisor stated that the checks were finally in for investigators who had not yet received reimbursement for the July 2016 conference. This confirmed a four-month delay for those investigators who spent money out of pocket to attend the required training.

The chief investigator continued to deviate from previous verbal or written policies she had set. One was the inconsistent dress code she both set and violated. Investigators were allowed to wear blue jeans and tactical gear cargo pants on some days but were verbally scolded for doing so on other days, with Stoneheart telling everyone they were professionals and needed to look like it.

Some days Stoneheart addressed the investigators in meetings and said casual wear, such as jeans, were okay on Fridays. She, however, dressed in jeans on other days of the week. The position as DA investigator demanded constant and sometimes sporadic courtroom appearances in the presence of judges, victims, and others who expected a professional appearance. Henry always presented himself at the highest level with business attire. He felt he was treated with disrespect because of his belief in high standards.

Performing work tasks was often difficult due to vehicle issues, which never seemed a priority. Some tasks and responsibilities, such as locating witnesses and serving subpoenas, were best completed with official vehicles not available outside of regular business hours. This could have been addressed with a take-home car policy for all. When this had been suggested in the past, the response was that there was no way to implement funding for fuel.

The failure to provide adequate funding for vehicles created bigger problems. Henry's normal routine after work was to wait for a shuttle outside the courthouse to drive himself to his personal vehicle. If the attorneys or investigators chose to not pay expensive fees to park their personal vehicle close to the office, they parked farther away and took the shuttle. Even if they were willing to pay the higher fees, those spots were made available from a waiting list, with some receiving special privileges to maneuver around it.

One day in November 2016, after finishing his day of work on a jury trial, Henry stood waiting for the bus in close proximity to the same jury he would testify in front of for that trial. He remained at a distance to ensure he did not speak about anything work-related in order to maintain integrity of the case. This also applied to attorneys who worked in the same courtrooms with jurors. There should never be any conversation between a juror, investigator, or prosecuting attorney, and the three should never be allowed to come together outside of the courtroom.

Running a shuttle system also resulted in potential safety issues. An attorney or investigator, both of whom could impact offenders for a lifetime, could be approached at the shuttle stop. Jurors were in full view of the entire courtroom, including any family members of the defendant who were attending a trial. If that jury rendered a guilty verdict and the defendant faced jail time, those family members or friends could easily find a juror standing outside the courthouse waiting for a shuttle bus. Several incidents occurred in high-profile cases involving gang violence or homicides when investigators were asked to escort attorneys, victims, and witnesses to private parking garages where their vehicles were parked. The escorts were necessary due to threats or even demeanors of those with interest to the defendant. These same concerns should have applied equally to investigators, attorneys, and jurors, who all stood on the public street waiting for shuttles to drive them to open parking lots.

Both District Attorney Rollins and Chief Investigator Stoneheart constantly expressed how budget shortfalls and lack of funds for salary increases had been created by the county as a whole. They advised that the county was not providing the necessary funding in the budget to meet operational needs, such as additional vehicle purchases and salary increases.

In December 2016, an employee asked Henry to participate in a petition to fight for reinstatement of pay from a March 2016 furlough imposed by the county. Henry did not understand why there was a request to sign a petition against being furloughed, when the district attorney had actually authorized the furlough. Henry thought the petition should have addressed the district attorney's negligence in managing his own budget rather than the county being at fault. Investigator Stoneheart held a meeting shortly after Henry was asked to sign the petition during which she confirmed that they should never have been furloughed. She passed the petition around for everyone to sign, adding that investigators who did not sign should not expect money if the petition was accepted. Henry did not sign because he felt it was not appropriate to sign a petition when budget revenue was mismanaged by the district attorney, who bore the responsibility for managing his budget. In March 2017 Henry came across an article reported by a local media source. It summarized that District Attorney Rollins accepted responsibility for the furlough of approximately two hundred employees, scheduled to be in effect for seventeen calendar days. It also highlighted that the furlough led to a dive in employee morale, multiple resignations, and delayed court trials. Rollins's reply was that the furlough was unnecessary, but that he misunderstood his budget and believed he needed to compensate for $846,000 of revenue that had already been deducted from his budget. Employees were furloughed for two days and were then advised that the furlough was ending. Henry received no updates related to the reinstatement of lost wages resulting from the furloughs.

In 2017, a fellow investigator told Henry he wanted to leave before another furlough occurred, and he felt more were coming based on the history of the office. During the same year, Henry spoke with another investigator about a feud which supposedly occurred between the district attorney and the finance staff of the county. He said a truce had been attempted at the beginning of the year. The attempt was unsuccessful after the district attorney requested a large amount of funds to make good on agreements to increase the salaries of employees who were promoted or promised raises. After many years of failed retention, one would expect this to have been addressed before it reached such a critical stage.

In June 2017, all the investigators in the office were addressed by District Attorney Rollins during a mandatory training session called by Chief Investigator Stoneheart. The discussion was related to motivating investigators in the midst of low office morale. Mention was made of salary increases for all investigators and additional increases throughout the year for individual performance to help with retention. District Attorney Rollins discussed a salary model that was used for some career positions authorized by the state departments. Although no salary amounts were mentioned by the DA, he confirmed one investigator in the office was currently working under a joint funding status between the state and the DA's office. The state was paying a percentage of the salary, and the office paid the remainder. The DA made it appear that the salary of the investigator was more attractive that the one the current investigators were receiving.

Other investigators, including Henry, were very aware of the investigator in question, who had recently retired with the county and was now working what was considered a part-time position, which allowed him to qualify for split funding with the state. There were no comments or responses to the DA's effort to explain the model used with the solitary position, as it did not seem to apply to how to increase the salary of all investigators. This continued to damage morale, as the model gave the perception that this investigator received a higher salary than the average investigator with the same experience or tenure. The investigator functioning under the dual salary compensation had functioned in the role for barely two years. Henry spoke with the investigator on several occasions, during which he confirmed the joint funding of his salary, although he never communicated an actual figure.

During the same June meeting, one of the investigators again proposed purchasing more vehicles to help with the financial gap from not receiving salary increases, in hopes of fostering more efficient performance. The investigator explained that being able to drive a county vehicle to and from work would save fuel and vehicle wear and tear, along with the monthly cost that some employees accrued for parking. The DA danced around the question but replied that he thought there was a committee of investigators working on the issue. This seemed another way of avoiding the issue, as Henry knew that those mentioned as the committee were no longer working at the DA's office. In fact, Henry had several conversations with the investigators prior to leaving, who confirmed proposals were presented to the DA several times, with no follow-up or steps taken to implement a program.

The running narrative was that the DA could operate his budget as he saw fit, and he seemed to do just that. The DA's ability to do as he wanted with his budget avoided scrutiny as long as he gave promotions or salary increases to individuals of his choosing. However, when budget shortfalls occurred, or concerns of other employees about providing pay increases or fair compensation to all were brought up, the DA seemed to point the finger at the county government for not providing additional budget funds or resources.

Just as Henry did every year, in July 2016 he presented a hardship letter stating the reasons he could not pay for training. His hardship letter was submitted in early May via email to the DA. After not getting a response for over a month, Henry followed up the first week of July with Rollin's administrative assistant and requested to speak to the DA about his letter.

According to the assistant, the DA could not meet with him because he had no availability, but she reported he was reviewing the hardship request. She would make him aware of Henry's inquiry about the request. He followed up again, after still getting no response and made a request for an update through the DA's office manager, who passed him on to the chief investigator.

Henry filed the hardship request each year because he needed it, but the process for approval changed every time. One year the responsibility belonged to Chief Stoneheart, and the next year it was the DA.

Finally, Stoneheart informed Henry that she would speak with the DA about the hardship. She added that this was somewhat last minute, with the conference scheduled to happen soon. However, Henry made the request in May and had made both Stoneheart and DA Rollins aware via email of his inability to pay for training up front, just as he did each year.

A few days before the conference, Stoneheart called to tell Henry that he was too late to get hardship funding and that it should have been handled earlier. Henry replied that based on that, he would be unable to attend. She stated she understood, but he should be prepared to face the consequences. His request two months prior was never acknowledged, and Henry was threatened with negative consequences.

After all attempts to make him responsible for their actions failed, Henry was called into the administrative office two days before the conference and provided with the necessary funds to attend.

To make matters worse, Stoneheart approached Henry during the conference, and in her condescending manner, she made it seem as though he should have extended gratitude and recognized her superiority over him.

"You could have called him and told him you got the funds," she said, talking about DA Rollins. "You didn't even say thank you!"

Henry made an effort to be professional and replied, "I'm sorry, Chief, but I did not want to continue to bother you."

"Well, you didn't have a problem calling him when you were trying to get it!" she countered.

She then asked if he thanked the DA for providing the funds. Staying professional, he explained that he had not seen him at the conference yet. She implied Henry should have been honored to have the leaders process funds related to his required job duties.

Toward the end of July 2017, another magic act was attempted involving the county finance department and specific employees. A coworker told Henry he received an increase in his salary due to the salary implemented to the newly hired investigators. He stated some of the new investigators, based upon experience, were receiving a starting salary which was greater than that of some senior investigators who were already occupying the position. The investigator also advised that this evaluation of the salary was done upon the county accessing the benefits and salaries of newly hired investigators compared to those of current investigators. However, Henry was not aware what process or policy was used to make the assessment, because no information was presented to all investigators to confirm this. Henry was also not aware of any additional investigators who benefited from the process explained by this investigator.

Once this information was discovered by Human Resources, it was deemed that anyone with the title of senior investigator had to be brought to that same salary level. If employees with similar qualifications and experience were being compensated at higher salaries, one would think that all investigators should be reviewed for a salary increase.

How would this impact an employee such as Henry, who never advanced above the base salary even after holding tenure, qualifications, and experience equivalent to or greater than others who had been promoted? The answer is, it didn't, and nothing changed. If employees have a right to salary adjustments, the administrative and finance divisions of the county should be responsible. Henry never saw an updated policy that supported these adjusted pay provisions and didn't know of any defined protocol to inquire what someone else's salary was so they could be compared. Henry had no confidence in the DA's office adopting a base standard of fairness. Based on his knowledge and belief, they promoted and gave salary increases without a defined process or justified means. This was yet another incident where Henry was depending on the transparency of a government agency to ensure fair pay standards were applied across the board when the circumstances applied, rather than the employee having to conduct their own independent research. However, Henry was also expecting the county, as an employer, to take the initial steps to ensure all employees were treated fairly.

CHAPTER 4

Leading by Fear

INVESTIGATORS AND OTHER EMPLOYEES repeatedly communicated their fear of being terminated if they did not perform to District Attorney Rollins's personal standards. Chief Investigator Stoneheart consistently told investigators either individually or in general meetings that they worked at the privilege of the DA and all positions were considered unclassified. This meant they were not considered to be under civil service standards, which in effect meant the employee could be terminated without cause. A civil service position would traditionally provide similar job protection as those employees who worked under a union contract. This meant that discipline or termination of an employee needed to be justifiable and explainable. Being reminded that you worked at the privilege of the DA was another way of imposing the fear of adverse actions if the leader's personal wishes were not met. The huge turnover seemed an indicator that many could no longer deal with the stressful demands of meeting these personal standards of leadership, and some communicated this to him personally.

During weekly Friday meetings, Stoneheart would constantly speak to the group with discouraging, unmotivating words when talking about their jobs. In early August 2016, she commented that several investigators appeared to be taking excessive sick leave but did not discuss any specific policy violations or examples. She said those who had not dedicated several years to their job should not be taking much time from work.

"I have dedicated over twenty-five years to the county," she explained. "And hell no, I'm not always sick when I use my time." She went on to say that when investigators invest the kind of time that she has with the county, then they can do that.

You would think that an employee's time should be treated with no less respect than that of the leader, who admitted to not only taking sick time, but not being sick when she took it.

The policy on sick leave was clear—employees who did not use sick leave before their employment ended would lose it. Stoneheart's own actions would not only show her improper use of sick leave, but also excessive use, based upon the county's sick leave policy, which did not make any exceptions for the chief investigator position. Traditionally, an employee planning retirement, resignation, or any other form of separation in their employment was required to surrender their remaining sick leave without pay. Even if other employees wanted to cover the deficit for a coworker, the policy allowed the transfer of only 240 hours. The donated leave could come only from the donor's compensatory time earned, vacation, or holiday pay, excluding accumulated sick leave hours. The donor of the leave was also required to maintain eighty hours of vacation leave themselves. Because of the obstacles of transferring paid time off, employees in need of hours found it difficult to get assistance. Most employees would have been more willing to donate sick leave hours than vacation hours, which were limited due to the short tenures of employment that many had. Sick leave hours could accumulate at a faster rate, because sick leave requested or used by staff members was taken less often than planned vacations. If an employee ends their employment, they will likely leave with more sick leave than vacation time due to the office discouraging the use of sick leave for anything but sickness. Selective standards existed for how the sick leave policy was interpreted and accepted. If an employee decided to end their employment with the county and had an excessive amount of sick leave remaining, they could not relinquish that time to another employee, as defined in the policy.

In October 2016 a meeting was held for newly hired investigators, but some who had been employed there for over a year were also asked to attend. This meeting involved training where investigators were presented a set of standard operating procedures. The contents were vague and only covered the minimum requirements of the job. These learn-as-you-go practices were an ongoing issue.

Chief Stoneheart made the decision of who could attend outside training apart from the policy training conducted at the DA's office. Some training programs charged fees, so several investigators were denied requests to attend and were told to resubmit for the next budget year. Some investigators were signing up and attending training during that same budget year and would be approved in spite of having no situations or conditions that justified the time or money spent on training. When investigators asked the chief for the criteria to attend training, she would confirm only that the training topic needed to be consistent with the employee's required duties and responsibilities. This was an inconsistent standard, as most training classes that were denied covered information related to the scope of their job description. It appeared that the chief investigator used her own personal criteria to make a decision as to who would receive paid training and who would be denied.

In several instances, investigators arrived at work and were told by Stoneheart that District Attorney Rollins was not in a good mood because he'd lost another employee to one of the surrounding county governments. He knew the challenges he faced in losing employees, but it seemed no effort to increase employee retention was ever made.

Of the approximately forty employees with whom Henry spoke personally prior to their resignations, only about eight left the office to pursue higher pay. They explained that not only did they have concerns with the lower pay in some positions, but their bigger concern was the manner in which pay raises and promotions were given. The employees consisted of attorneys, investigators, paralegals, and victim advocates. The others voiced that they were seeking to be treated with respect and they desired good leadership without control and intimidation. This was not much to ask, but appeared to be more than the district attorney, chief investigator, and those involved in management of the county government were willing to provide.

Each year, it seemed more and more citizens were seeking involvement in the decisions and actions of their government by attempting to establish their own city and municipality. Many formed their own cities out of frustration. These frustrations included police services, bad financial management, and a slew of unethical practices created by county leaders. Over the years, it was believed that organizing one's own jurisdiction would ensure better government services. Cities and counties would always be under the guidance of city officials, district attorneys, and those who commission counties, but the DA's office appeared to be hiring "temp workers" rather than building careers. Employees will always have personal reasons for leaving a career. It is very rare in the criminal justice profession that an employee becomes certified as an investigator or licensed as an attorney and then tries a totally new profession. None of the investigators who spoke with Henry about their resignations stated they were pursuing a new profession. They were simply transitioning to other DA offices. They expressed that it was not the position or the profession that they were escaping, but rather the controlling leadership of this particular environment.

It is one thing to intimidate employees and impose your will against them to complete day-to-day operations, but it's something else to allow that behavior to impact financial decisions. At the end of January 2017, as Henry processed a case for trial, a discussion occurred regarding out-of-state witnesses. Henry spoke with his assigned attorney who was still finding her way with the logistics of the county court operations in the DA's office. She instructed him when she wanted the witnesses to fly in, but there were no reasons for them to testify the day they arrived. She feared issues would occur that would prevent the witnesses being present when needed to testify for trial.

These concerns were common since defense attorneys would request reset dates, which were not always provided to prosecuting attorneys. This process seemed one-sided. One judge stated the burden was upon the prosecution, yet the defendant in the case was the most inconvenienced.

These delays caused victims and witnesses for the prosecution to become frustrated and detached, ultimately creating difficulties for the attorneys as well as the investigators. The transportation of witnesses and victims who lived out of state was costly and had to be accounted for. Many of them flew commercial and were told to return home with no resolution.

Another incident in early February 2017 occurred during trial preparation with attempts to get a witness to travel from Florida. The procedure to have an out-of-state witness comply with the case was not followed. The protocol was for the attorney to draft an order and communicate that order to a judge in the state where the witness lived, justifying the need to have that witness travel out of state. A witness has the right to explain why they are unable to appear before a judge, who then makes the decision to either excuse them or order their appearance. This process was not followed, either in this case or in other cases Henry worked.

This posed only an inconvenience to the DA's office. The attorneys would say they simply did not have time to navigate the protocol. Unfortunately for witnesses and victims, if they experienced difficulties traveling out of state, they would be left with no options unless they knew the procedures. If the victims and witnesses were unable to make the trip, the defense team could suggest their cases be dismissed, rendering no justice for the victim. Although the victims had concerned interests in their own cases, some would inform investigators that there were too many delays in getting the trial started. Others explained that the prosecuting attorneys would sometimes request them at the last minute, not allowing them to give their employers enough notice or allow time to arrange for childcare. Witnesses had the same challenges. If not related to the victim, they may have less interest in coming to another state to testify. A large number of witnesses expressed that they were not compensated by their jobs, and only received twenty-five dollars pay from the court system each day. Even the professional witnesses, such as law enforcement and medical staff, became frustrated as cases were reset multiple times with no explanation, causing both their professional and personal lives to be affected negatively.

The attorney assigned to work the case instructed Henry to make flight arrangements for the witness, but a week prior, the witness stated he could not miss work to travel out of state. Henry provided this information to the attorney, who instructed him again to make flight arrangements. When a witness presented issues with appearing out of state, the process began for an out-of-state witness order. Once the flight was arranged, Henry called the witness to provide him the information. He told Henry he'd been excused by the assigned attorney, who confirmed this was true. This lack of communication was common in the DA's office.

Many of the attorneys Henry worked with communicated their discomfort in not being able to excuse witnesses, even those not vital to the case, without the approval of the district attorney. District Attorney Rollins had a personal standard of wanting every witness to be subpoenaed and appear for trial without accepting any input from the assigned attorneys, if the witnesses were relevant. When investigators communicated their struggles with attorneys of getting nonessential witnesses to come to court, they were advised that the DA wanted all witnesses in court. As an investigator, Henry understood that some witnesses would provide a duplication of information relative to a case. If one of those witnesses were uncooperative, it made no sense to force them to come to trial if they could not add much valuable input to a case. Forcing them to come risked them being disgruntled on the witness stand. A disgruntled testimony could be seen as dishonest, which could work in the favor of the defendant by making a potential juror disbelieve the witness's testimony. The attorney made no attempt to inform him that this witness could be excused. The nonrefundable flight cost the county $320.00 of taxpayer money. There are no figures compiled to show how much the county lost each year for cancelled flights. The flight arrangements requested or cancelled at the last minute were nonrefundable.

The attorneys were under tremendous stress when not allowed to make day-to-day decisions on cases, such as determining which witnesses were important and which could be excused. There are times when delegating authority is important and beneficial, but this authority was often not granted to the attorneys. The continuing efforts of the DA to eliminate the case attorneys from deciding which witnesses they needed seemed to create never-ending difficulties with witness cooperation. The controlling efforts of the DA's office appeared more damaging than any expertise it had to offer.

CHAPTER 5

✳

Victims and Witnesses
for Life

THE DISTRICT ATTORNEY'S OFFICE frequently compelled victims and witnesses to testify in court, not just for cases they were involved in, but also for other cases with the same defendants. These are called "similar transaction cases."

These victims and witnesses would say they felt harassed by investigators to come to court, and were told if they didn't comply, they faced some tough consequences. In one case, a young lady refused to be a part of a sexual assault trial where the accused person was a defendant in her trial. Countless hours were spent attempting to locate her, and investigators were to serve a material witness arrest warrant if she did not make herself available. The material witness warrants were just as they sound. When a person was considered an important and material part of the case, they could be held until trial, or required to be available. After major efforts and resources of investigators were used, the witness was located and made to appear before the courts to provide a testimony for the pending case related to her similar experiences.

In Henry's opinion, the case would not have suffered by the former victim refusing to testify, as she was not the primary victim in the case. Any criminal case should be able to stand on the merits of the accusations and the evidence. When a witness is considered a similar transaction witness, such as a victim, the expectation by the prosecuting attorney is for the victim to confirm that similar events happened to them as well, caused by the same accused person involved in the current case. Even though similar events may have occurred with the victim of a past case, there was nothing that the past victim would testify to which would confirm that the accused defendant in the current case was guilty. The old case could only attempt to bolster the current case against the defendant. The previous victim explained that she did not want to hurt her current relationship by opening up old wounds of a sexual assault.

In another incident, a victim was placed in harm's way by a prosecuting attorney who lacked experience in sexual assault cases. The victim was a homeless woman who agreed to testify even after expressing a fear of doing so. She was placed in a hotel as a precaution. The lead prosecuting attorney made a dangerous error by providing the victim's information to the defense attorney, including her phone number and the hotel name and room number. The only legal requirement in processing the case, unless the witness is under strict witness protection, is to provide names of expected witnesses to the defense attorney and nothing else. The witness later had to be moved for her safety.

The victim/witness advocacy program, designed for guidance and support, was not beneficial in many cases. The advocates themselves had very low morale and complained of being overworked and severely underpaid. In 2018 another concern arose which Henry believed would negatively impact victims of crimes. The state placed an amendment to Article 1 of its constitution by adding a paragraph to the state's Marsy's Law. Marsy's Law was established in November 2008 by Henry T. Nicholas III under Proposition 9, The California Victims' Bill of Rights Act of 2008. Henry Nicholas fought to have the law added to the state's Bill of Rights after his sister, a bright University of California Santa Barbara student, was killed by her boyfriend. The defendant was later released on bond, where he encountered the victim's mother in a local market just a week after the funeral. This drove Henry Nicholas to fight for specific rights to be considered and added to his state's Bill of Rights. Several other states adopted Marsy's Law as well. When the 2018 bill was voted on and approved in the same year, it presented specific changes for victims which also changed how advocates in the office would assist them. Paragraph 111 stated the following:

(a) For the purpose of this paragraph, a victim shall be considered an individual against whom a crime has allegedly been perpetrated, including crimes of delinquent acts. Such victim shall be accorded the utmost dignity and respect and shall be treated fairly by the criminal justice system of the state and all agencies and departments that serve such system. When the crime is one against or involving the person of the victim or is a felony property crime, such victim shall be afforded the following rights: (1) The Right upon request to reasonable, accurate and timely notice of any scheduled court proceedings involving the alleged act or changes of the scheduling of such proceedings; (2) The Right upon request to reasonable, accurate and timely notice of the arrest, release, or escape of the accused.

The state's Crime Bill of Rights, when compared to the 2018 amendment, defined that a victim had the right to information of proceedings free from unreasonable delay; to reasonable, accurate, and timely notice of arrest warrant actions for the accused; the arrest; the terms of prohibited contact with the victim by the accused; and any escape from custody or the release of the accused. In comparison, the 2018 amendment appeared to shift the criminal justice system's duty and responsibility to notify victims of vital information which could affect them, perhaps forever, by implementing the terms "upon request." It now became the responsibility of the victims to not only be aware of the amendment, but also to pursue those who had such information. If a victim followed up to receive such information and was unsuccessful in making contact with anyone, it could place them in harm's way if a defendant was released or escaped from custody.

Many victims and witnesses are uncooperative because they fear retaliation—against them, their families, their friends, and others connected to them. In September 2016 a trial was set to start, and the witness who was once available to testify could not be reached by the lead investigator. Chief Investigator Stoneheart called a meeting to assist with locating the witness.

The supervisor of the homicide division stated that he made an error by declining to pursue a warrant and hold the witness until trial. The witness was difficult and not responding to previous requests to come forward. The witness's mother said she feared her son testifying, and so did he. The supervisor wanted to place the witness in a hotel until he was needed but decided not to because of limited occupancy for the last-minute request. A low-occupancy hotel was needed to ensure only a limited number of people would come in contact with the witness. Such contact would compromise safety. Due to the hotel challenges, the supervisor allowed the witness to stay with his girlfriend.

When the witness was needed the next day, he went missing. The supervisor of the homicide division reached out to the witness's mother, who became extremely upset with the situation. She felt the office had put her son in harm's way. The chief investigator assigned all the investigators to look for the witness. Henry was sent to the witness's last known address, his aunt's residence, and met with the witness's mother, grandmother, and aunt.

When homicide cases were prepared for trial, it was common for witnesses to receive direct and indirect threats of violence if they testified. Witnesses usually gave minimal information on the threats and believed they were safer facing the consequences of not testifying. The family believed the office did not do enough to provide a safe environment for the witness, regardless of what the witness wanted.

Some of the cases Henry investigated did not appear strong enough to prosecute. It seemed easier for inexperienced or overwhelmed prosecutors to use the efforts of a witness, whether credible or not, to convict a case as opposed to firmly expressing the option to dismiss the case. Numerous prosecutors expressed concerns with telling the DA they did not have a good case. Some just wanted to gain experience in the DA's office and move on.

A random selection of cases always seemed to be valued more than others. Long delays frustrated victims and witnesses. They were contacted multiple times with updates and told the case was going to trial, and then it would be delayed, dismissed, or end in a plea bargain. The witnesses who voiced their concerns to Henry expressed that they felt the resolutions should have been conducted and communicated to them on a consistent basis. Some of the prosecuting attorneys had a one-hour on-call system in place for the professional witnesses, such as police officers, medical witnesses, or experts in certain fields of criminology. The on-call witnesses could be contacted an hour before they were actually needed to testify. The office did have a standard operating policy, however, which could have allowed other witnesses to be placed in an on-call status, which could have help to reduce the frustration. Witnesses expressed concern about having to leave their places of employment several times, even though laws were designed to prevent any action against a witness for court appearances. Witnesses told Henry several times that they did not live in the real world, faced with trying to keep a job and fulfilling court demands. Even if the case finally reached trial, the delays were sometimes so long that witnesses would forget information, change their stories, or simply refuse to continue with the process. Investigators were then tasked with communicating this to the prosecutor and obtaining a warrant.

This was even more disturbing with young victims, who stated numerous times they could not remember the incident. It was extremely painful to watch minority families and victims of low economic status being treated as second-class citizens by the criminal justice system.

In October 2016 Henry found himself involved in a three-day email battle involving one of the police department's special victim's units that Henry's DA prosecuted cases for. He involved his direct supervisor and the assigned attorney's supervisor as well. Henry's goal was to get a vital forensic interview set up with a young victim after the police department who was prosecuting the case, the Special Victims Division, failed to do so. Although Henry worked aggressively to meet this goal, the investigator for the division claimed she was busy with other things and it would be a month before she could schedule the forensic interview. When Henry suggested options to get someone to fill the gap, he received emails from her supervisor, to whom she'd forwarded the message.

He replied, based upon his previous narrative about the case in his independent interview, that it appeared the child had been reluctant to talk. The Special Victims Unit at the police department cannot compel any child to cooperate.

Henry followed up by saying that the Special Victims Unit's expertise was not in conducting child forensic interviews, and the decisions and techniques should be left up to the forensic specialist. Henry informed the unit's supervisor via email that he wanted to discuss this issue. The police supervisor made an appointment for a week later, then cancelled the day it was scheduled, saying an incident had come up. He did not provide another day to meet.

To Henry, it appeared that three different levels of the justice system—the police department special victim's supervisor, the district attorney investigations supervisor, and the deputy district attorney for crimes involving women and children, were not acting in the best interest of an innocent child victim. Extremely disappointed, Henry felt the leaders of the respective departments should have done more for a child victim. Advocating for child victims is an important role in the criminal justice system, because many times the accused are actually close family members or even parents of the victim. Therefore, the criminal justice system should be the voice and line of defense for the young victim. The case was already facing a delay of a year and a half. Evidence such as a forensic interview for a child victim is extremely important, as the defense attorney assigned to the case will often ask if the interview took place and question the results and the expertise of the interview. The delay or lack of an interview also creates difficulty for the child witness, as many of the young victims have trouble recalling the events. Henry received no feedback from either the leaders who had knowledge of the forensic interview concerns, or the assigned attorney, in regard to how they wished to proceed. Even if Henry had taken the initiative to reach out to the forensic interview specialist to schedule an interview for the child, the assigned attorney and the leaders needed to determine how they wanted to proceed. The people in charge of getting justice for victims never seemed to understand the impact high turnover had on these innocent young crime victims.

In a different case in November 2016 Henry attempted to make contact with a young victim's aunt, who was also the primary caretaker, to tell her that their case was being assessed for a possible trial date. She thought the case was no longer being considered since she had not had any response from the DA's office. Like Henry had on many occasions, he again apologized on behalf of the office. She asked him if the same prosecutor was still assigned to the case, and Henry explained that a new one had been assigned. She was very upset and could not believe this had not been relayed to her. Even with all the apologies and empathy Henry extended, she was simply unwilling to accept the negligence displayed by the office.

Management by the chief investigator, supervising attorney, and advocate supervisor in keeping the victim and witnesses informed was a constant concern expressed by the victims and witnesses. This could have easily been managed by conducting adequate transition of case files. The attorneys' assignments changed frequently from one courtroom to another, and some type of exchange of information was needed between attorneys, investigators, and victim/witness advocate staff, all of whom conducted work on the case. Updates covering what work had been completed, what was outstanding, and what updates and notifications had been given to the victim about what was occurring should have been provided to the new staff working on the case. With no required protocol, it was left up to the individual attorney, investigator, or witness advocate to formally bring the new person receiving the case up to speed. Although some staff did leave notes on actual documents in file, some information was still limited and vague. Prosecutors, investigators, and advocates would sometimes resign, which resulted in even less desire to make sure case information was updated, communicated, and documented. The victim/witness advocates had a general policy in the office to provide victims with case updates every sixty and ninety days, but that too was inconsistent and not enforced by the supervising staff. The advocates also expressed that the failure to make contact with many victims was due to the high turnover and large case volume. Even when the advocates made their best efforts to reach victims, which many did, without a team effort from the prosecutors they would face challenges in keeping victims totally informed. The advocates had the ability to review electronic notes and documents left by attorneys and investigators in the case file. However, the attorneys would sometimes have discussions with defense attorneys and meetings with the district attorney, and the information was not shared with advocates or investigators. The attorneys would discuss only that they met with the DA but would not offer any details or document the information in the file. The information withheld would sometimes be the same information the advocates and investigators would later be expected to relay to witnesses and victims. The information would consist of additional witnesses, needed or not; hearing and trial date resets; or additional evidence with limited turnaround time needed from the investigator. Some information related to case updates could be obtained by the advocates or the investigators attending court proceedings with the attorney before trial, such as evidence suppression hearings to exclude evidence or calendar call events. However, both the advocate and the investigator could be tasked with meeting other deadlines requested by the attorney, which separated them from the courtroom. The timely communication of the case then rested on the shoulders of the assisted attorney. During general investigator meetings, they were made aware that they'd be moving to a standard to overcome communication concerns that would include scheduling team meetings involving the case attorney, the advocate, and the investigator, but they were never consistent due to other case demands or attorney conflicts. When daily communication failed and victims were left totally unaware of updates on their cases, they often communicated that the office did not seem to care or was no longer interested in the case. It only takes a phone call to build or maintain the confidence of the victims or witnesses, and this practice creates the best opportunity for compliance when the individuals are needed to testify or adjust to changes in their trial scheduling.

Later the same month as Henry talked with a prosecutor, they pondered the large number of employees resigning their positions. They also talked about the stress prosecutors faced pursuing cases where evidence was limited or facts inconsistent.

Some defendants had convictions in other jurisdictions, which resulted in substantial sentences for serious felonies. Prosecutors would request permission from the DA to plea bargain lighter sentences, and these penalties would be added to whatever the defendant was facing in other jurisdictions. These requests were presented to victims for their opinions, and many victims agreed to what the prosecutor was presenting. DA Rollins did not approve of plea bargaining as a general standard. It was common for prosecuting attorneys to ask the victims what type of resolution they would like to see take place with the case. If they were okay with the defendant plea bargaining to a lower sentence, it would normally be presented to the district attorney. However, when the DA failed to consider plea bargaining the case, the victims would voice their displeasure. The victims often questioned the attorneys and investigators as to why they had to relive the incidents by going to trial and perhaps see the accused person set free. Even though Henry understood the concerns, he did not have an answer that could reassure them. Some of these same witnesses became problematic with the trial process, making themselves unavailable to testify. Although plea bargaining could have been beneficial in reducing the risk of uncooperative witnesses and victims and save the costs of a trial, the final decision always seemed to rest with the DA, regardless of the risk.

The average person may think victims would like to see their cases go to trial, but many of them only want justice, period. This allows them to start the process of healing and avoids them reliving the pain again and again with delayed trials.

In one case, a prosecutor sent Henry several requests to locate victims and witnesses of different cases that all involved the defendant. Most were in his jurisdiction, but some were in others. Henry was asked to be sensitive with these witnesses and treat them with kid gloves when serving subpoenas. When Henry inquired if there were any particular concerns, the prosecutor expressed exhaustion and could not deal with another trial delay.

The delay would only be a problem in this case if DA Rollins denied the prosecutors' requests to consider a plea bargain with a lighter sentence. The defendant had recently been convicted in another jurisdiction. Even though all were professional investigators and attorneys with the most knowledge of the case, their opinions were not valued by the DA.

A local news station ran a story at the end of December 2016 that covered a traffic accident fatality from July 2012 involving a police officer, where a victim's spouse wanted answers regarding the police officer's punishment. The officer had been fired by his department and was later convicted of homicide by vehicle and reckless driving. The terms of the conviction were ten years, with two years served in jail, but the jail time would only be served on the weekends. After one year of serving weekends, the former officer was transferred to a jail closer to his home. The deceased victim's husband expressed that the actions were insulting to his wife's memory and referred to it as "special treatment." He also expressed in the article that no one even considered notifying him.

The husband of the deceased found out through the office's victim advocate that the officer had been transferred from the county jail to the jail in his hometown to finish his sentence. The news staff attempted to get a response from the jail staff and the DA's office, but no explanation was provided. Although neither the DA's office nor the jail facility who housed the defendant had a legal obligation to contact the family of the deceased in regard to the transfer, the sentencing conviction itself appeared beyond explanation. Under the state's Victim's Bill of Rights, the state and government entities—which include law enforcement agencies, prosecuting attorney, correctional facilities, and pardon and parole board—only needed to meet a specific guideline. In this case, there was nothing that covered notifying the victim's family of custody transfers, as it was neither a release nor escape. The actions of the justice system appeared immoral, as if they were operating under the standards and did not have consideration for the deceased victim's husband. It seemed bad enough that the sentencing allowed jail time to be served only on weekends, and Henry also felt it disrespectful to the family of the deceased to not publicly explain why the transfer occurred. The failure to explain why the transfer was allowed further supported the family's concern that a law enforcement officer had received special treatment in the criminal justice system. Until someone took substantial steps to create change in how victims and witnesses are treated and informed by the DA's office, they would wait on the next negative encounter with the criminal justice system.

Henry witnessed one incident after another where victims did not receive true justice. In February 2017, Henry worked on a trial with a prosecutor who was undergoing tremendous stress after wrapping up an additional trial in the same week. The new trial was in the vital stage of selecting a jury.

Henry spoke to the prosecutor and asked, "If they are still in the middle of finishing up this trial, how would they have time to complete the jury selection process for a new trial starting up?"

She responded that the second chair attorney working on the case, who was also her deputy supervisor, would select her jury. Henry thought it very interesting to allow a different attorney to select a jury for a trial since the primary attorney needed to establish a foundation and rapport with the jury. The adversarial process of the criminal justice system relies on both the prosecutor and defense attorney's abilities to connect with the jury. Even though a jury can be selected by any attorney, the opportunity to connect with each juror cannot be discounted.

The trial resulted in a "not guilty" verdict. The lead prosecutor said she learned a valuable lesson and would never again allow someone else to pick her jury. She also highlighted the fact that most of the jurors had no desire to speak with her about their decision. Then the judge stated that the case was too old, which lowered the odds of the state winning. His perception was that the prosecutors were unable to put quality efforts into preparing cases because of the high volume and inability to resolve them through other means, such as plea bargains.

When a person's ability to receive justice sits on the ballots of others, the responsibilities should not be taken lightly, and should be granted time to assess negative outcome rather than treating incidents as merely the cost of doing business.

During the week of April 17, 2017, Henry was given the task of locating a sexual assault victim. When Henry finally found her through information provided by her mother, she was not doing well physically and was losing her fight with drug addiction. Henry eventually managed to get her to speak with him over the phone.

She said she needed help with her addiction and preferred therapy, so Henry told her he would work on getting her some resources. It is very important that victims are okay throughout the trial process and beyond. Though Henry immediately informed the staff members needed to assist—a victim's advocate, the case attorney, managers, and supervisors—he never received any assistance or an action plan from the management staff, so he was unable to give the victim any positive solutions. Henry communicated with the mother, who advised she would reach out to her daughter and assist as much as her finances would allow. Unfortunately, the resources provided by the office to assist victims and witnesses appeared limited, especially with no scheduled trial date. When a witness was scheduled to testify for a trial and needed to be placed in a hotel until needed, required paperwork had to be signed off on by the assigned case attorney, their supervisor, and the chief investigator. However, the victim advocate staff took the lead when providing resources such as shelter or any temporary housing resources.

A couple months later, Henry received a phone call from the mother of the victim. She told him her daughter still needed help. The case was set for trial in May but was postponed due to jury selection issues with the county, which were unrelated to this case. The victim was homeless and needed somewhere to stay. The mother, who lived in another state, did not have the resources to help her daughter and reported her daughter became combative if they were in the same house.

Henry then spoke with the victim by phone and told her he would come pick her up and attempt to find her a shelter. Henry brought her back to his office and found a victim's advocate staff member who reached out to several shelters but was unsuccessful. The supervisor of the program knew of no other resources. After spending eight hours trying to find a place for the woman, he came away empty. He contacted the mother to make her aware that he was again unable to help, but Henry could get the victim a bus ticket to her mother's location, even though the victim did not want that. Despite their previous issues, the mother agreed to let her come. It was unfortunate that no safe place could be provided to the victim.

Each day, investigators would spend hours, sometimes days, attempting to locate victims and witnesses for trial. This time however, Henry had the victim in the county, but had no place for her to go. Now he would be faced with trying to locate her for trial in a different state if things did not work out with her mother. In the past, the DA's office had provided hotel rooms for witnesses and victims during trial. That would have been an option in this case, but the trial hadn't started and didn't even have a date set yet. There was no policy in place for special circumstances such as this. Henry never understood why the county expressed willingness to help victims, then suddenly had no answers when the victims were at their lowest.

In June 2017, Henry found himself at the center of yet another challenging issue. He was asked by a supervisor to assist in obtaining the DNA of a victim through a legal search warrant but had been provided with very limited details of the incident. He had a verbal summary of the facts but no incident report to confirm them. The incident involved a 9-1-1 call with an open line that came from a residence. The open line revealed a statement made by a male, which police believed was evidence of a sexual assault, in which a woman was not consenting to sexual intercourse. Henry was not made aware of what charges were made against anyone or to establish enough probable cause to request a DNA search warrant from an uncooperative person when no one had reported a crime. A sexual assault charge must show evidence of the assault, including but not limited to DNA, to support such charges. When the assault involves sexual intercourse, DNA testing is completed in the form of a rape kit conducted by a sexual assault nurse examiner (SANE) nurse. This nurse is specially trained in the collection of forensic evidence, which may identify elements of a sexual assault. Search warrants are sometimes requested for evidence, such as saliva swabs from victims and the accused, to compare to DNA collected from a crime scene or from a sexual assault rape kit of a victim, to confirm DNA matches related to the sexual assault. In this case, they had none of these things. The challenge was that the victim was expressing that no crime was either reported or had occurred. The greatest challenge was subjecting a person to a search of their DNA against their will. The laws of the state highlighted that prosecution can be pursued without the assistance of the victim, who, if not cooperative, is considered just another witness. However, the ultimate concern will still be the obtaining of vital evidence from a victim. Based upon the limited information Henry received, he could not confirm or deny a crime in order to request a search warrant from a judge. The attempts to compel someone to a search of their DNA to support an alleged, unreported crime seems controlling, unfair, and unconstitutional.

The goal of every prosecution should be to provide justice for victims and safety for the community. Obtaining DNA from an unwilling person to support a crime would not provide justice or protect the community. Without a supportive victim, the DA's office appeared to operate with agendas other than justice.

Henry explained to the supervisor that he was unable to apply for a DNA search warrant for facts that were not clear or supported by documentation. He did, however, suggest that a hearing be set up that allowed the woman to appear before a judge to discuss why the DNA was needed. There was no response to his suggestion, and Henry was unfamiliar with the disposition of the incident because he was not the assigned investigator but only the one asked by the supervisor to draft and request a search warrant. It was unclear if his suggestions were considered or acted upon by the supervisor who requested him to obtain the woman's DNA. Henry was never presented with a police report upon requesting assistance, nor was he advised of what actual charges were alleged against this accused person.

It's understandable that victims and witnesses may become fearful, intimidated, and unwilling to come forward. If the courts are going to allow testimonies to be used as engines to prosecute, Henry believed those testimonies should be given freely and willingly to avoid exaggeration or falsehood. The process of compelling victims and witnesses to testify in court is constitutional judiciary article (111) of the constitution. This article states that a judicial subpoena (which defines that the person named in the subpoena is in control of documents or physical evidence such as testimony) is needed to view or obtain such evidence. The subpoena process was a part of the adopted Judiciary Act of 1789, a United States federal statute adopted on September 24, 1789. The judicial power of the United States was vested in one Supreme Court, along with lower courts. However, during his employment at the DA's office, the process of choosing which witnesses and victims to enforce those laws upon appeared unfair and seemed to target those with less knowledge of the justice system. The treatment of victims also varied depending on economic status and demographics. Henry believed the way victims and witnesses are treated during the criminal justice process is how they will accept the responsibility of performing their civic duty as a witness and as a victim for their case. Each time this is compromised, it carries the risk that guilty offenders will be set free.

CHAPTER 6

The Legal Conflict

IN THE CRIMINAL JUSTICE SYSTEM, it is important to hire and retain the most qualified applicants since the profession is faced with a great many challenges. Government agencies, such as police departments and DA offices, often share the aftereffects of not hiring the best applicants.

The police officer who makes an arrest must eventually present the case to the DA's office to be prosecuted. It then gets turned over to an investigator. If both agencies are without highly trained and qualified employees, it could lead to wrongful convictions or failed justice for the victims. The DA's office carried its own weight of concerns with prosecuting cases, aside from assisting police departments.

An investigator with the DA's office helps prepare a case for trial by meeting several deadlines for information requests, such as court orders, search warrants, and other legal documents. Failure to execute these tasks successfully could result in a guilty defendant being set free.

During the interview phase of his own hiring, Henry was given a case file and timed while he reviewed several documents to determine what should be included to reach a successful prosecution. Henry wondered whether this process continued to be used with applicants after he began working there. In addition to the face-to-face interview, part of the hiring process was very important in assessing whether a candidate could meet the requirements of the position, as it would assess the candidate's ability to apply their experience. This step of the process was also able to determine what training opportunities would be beneficial to the candidate, if offered a position.

With over twelve years of experience in an investigative capacity, Henry was quite familiar with the characteristics of a well-rounded investigator. In addition to being thorough, prompt, and detailed, it was imperative one be familiar with the Fourth Amendment of the United States Constitution. This knowledge allows a police officer or investigator to engage the rules and legal means to search people, places, and items when it is believed a crime has occurred. Before any legal search is conducted, law enforcement personnel must explain to a judge or judicial official why such a search is needed. The judge determines if there is legal cause to conduct searches or enter into the privacy of citizens. This process is vital because it provides the foundation to establish evidence against an accused person. It could also produce evidence that would free an accused person.

The DA's office had a computer network with resources and information, viewable by all investigators in the office. There, investigators could find several forms and drafts of documents needed to perform their duties. This tool was meant to review and to use as a guide for legal documents such as search warrants and courts orders but are not meant to be used as cut-and-paste documents.

This access allowed investigators to use work done by other investigators and to change only the names, locations, and a few details. This in turn would be presented to a judge to be signed as a search warrant. This common approach gave the perception that search warrants or court orders are one-size-fits-all legal documents, rather than documents that contain all original words of the investigator. This can lead to incorrect information being included in the request, such as incidents that may not have occurred, or not to that degree. Going before a judge to have the document signed requires the law enforcement professional to swear or affirm that all information enclosed is true to the best of their knowledge.

These procedures were not only common practice in the DA's office, but many investigators did not understand that a tool accessed for guidance could also produce conflict. Many also never had formal training on writing and securing search warrants and court orders. Some investigators would get other investigators to write the warrant for them and then present the warrant themselves. This is not only unlawful, but it also places the whole criminal case in jeopardy. Due to lack of knowledge and training, the office was placing investigators in situations where they were rubber-stamping cases and going through the motions. Several new investigators approached him for assistance in writing search warrants.

In 2014, a senior assistant attorney asked Henry to have a blanket sent to the crime lab for DNA testing. He was also asked to get a DNA sample from the defendant, who was detained in the county jail. He wanted to have both DNA samples compared as soon as possible so the results could return around the same time and be ready for trial. Henry informed him that, based upon the rules of evidence comparison and the Fourth Amendment rights of the accused, he needed to wait until there was a positive result for male DNA before he would have legal cause to request a sample from the accused. The attorney accepted this but was not happy.

In most circumstances, investigators in the office would have immediately honored the request by the attorney because they weren't familiar with search and seizure processes. This was a prime example of the office valuing results over legal requirements. American justice has always been said to represent legal and fair processes—or has it?

In January 2017, a mandatory meeting was called to discuss an operation that would take place. The group was briefed on a high-profile case with a suspicious death that was being handled by the office. The plan was to perform surveillance on the suspect and a woman who may have been his mistress. It was set to run for possibly two weeks, around the clock, in the hope of obtaining stronger evidence to support the charges of murder against the suspect. The incident occurred in 2016. The accused was in the backseat of an SUV, driven by a friend, with his wife in the passenger front seat. According to the accused's account of the events, he had a firearm sitting in his lap that accidentally went off when he dozed off to sleep. He stated the firearm was exposed due to his fears of being carjacked. The initial charges were felony involuntary manslaughter and misdemeanor reckless conduct. The manslaughter charge defines that the death of another was caused by the accused without intent or malice to do so; however, the act would still be illegal, such as pointing and discharging a firearm at another without justification. Reckless conduct charges are defined as an accused person who causes bodily harm to another or places them at an unjustified risk of danger. However, when the case was presented to a grand jury for review, the charges were upgraded to malice murder, to include other related charges.

The suspect lived, or was known to be, at several different residential addresses. Instructions were to follow the suspect and the alleged mistress and take photographs of their presence together. Everyone in the room was asked collectively if they were familiar with following someone or conducting surveillance. No one in the room verbalized a lack of such knowledge or experience. There was no formal training provided to investigators on how to successfully conduct such a sensitive and unsafe operation. When an investigation such as surveillance is conducted, it often involves working in an undercover capacity to avoid detection by those being watched. The assignment also has those conducting the investigation appearing as an average citizen, lacking identifying law enforcement or authority features. If an attack or force is used against those conducting the investigation, the accused could easily justify that they believed they were being stalked or were the subject of a potential attack such as robbery or carjacking, as the accused in this case alleged to have happened, which led to his wife's death. Proper surveillance conduct also ensured proper distance was maintained, which would help prevent coming under attack by those being investigated. The fact that this was a murder case was enough to demand the highest level of safety by those involved. But no safety plan was in place in the event that the detail was compromised or safety concerns arose.

Some of the assigned locations were outside of the county. Some investigators, including Henry, asked if they needed to call those jurisdictions as a courtesy to let them know they were conducting an operation in their area in case they needed assistance involving safety. However, they did not receive any instructions to do so.

Within many law enforcement agencies, procedures exist for law enforcement entities to communicate with one another for what is known as "deconfliction." This was a process of communicating or obtaining a confidential number from other agencies, primarily in the jurisdiction where the investigation is headed, in an effort to ensure that law enforcement resources are not targeting the same persons. If agencies of the criminal justice system encounter one another and are unable to identify each other, there is no way to determine which normal citizens are in authority. This could lead to deadly force being used against criminal justice staff. Even the instructions on how to take photographs of the targeted subjects were not precise or detailed. There were also no instructions of what to do with photographs that could eventually be used as evidence. The photographer must be prepared to testify as to why and how the photographs were taken, as well as explain how the evidence was processed and stored. Most crime scenes that are processed for evidence to support criminal charges undergo a formal process, traditionally carried out by the first responding law enforcement person. The process involves collecting and packaging the evidence and completing a paper or electronic documentation known as the "chain of custody" information. This information provides a description of evidence, the location it came from, and the date and time of collection. The information must also display every person and location which causes the evidence to change from one person or location to another. Evidence is routinely maintained at a secured location until there is a legal means to access it, such as evidence hearings or the actual trial. In this situation, there were no clear instructions of what type of camera would be used, where it would come from, and how the evidence would be maintained. Many law enforcement agencies have a division that exists only to process and maintain evidence, and which are provided with the necessary equipment to process evidence. However, Henry's office had no such division to process an evidence scene, only an area to store evidence obtained from the agency prosecuting the case. The office had an investigator tasked with maintaining evidence from closed cases, which could be requested for appeals or for cases that were actively on trial and evidence requested. This investigator could have been tasked with managing the entire process, but this was not a general practice, as the investigator would say that he had his own cases to manage, as he too was assigned to prepare cases for trial for other attorneys. When investigators attempted to get clarity on how photographing would be conducted during the investigation, Chief Investigator Stoneheart advised only to stand by, and she would provide an update once the briefing of the assignment was over. Henry did not receive any additional updates on how the process would proceed.

The DA's office seemed to conduct business in ways that were convenient for them, rather than considering the overall needs of the justice system.

Chief Investigator Stoneheart spoke about the operation and how she knew the assignment and expectations were new to many. If there were any questions about how to perform the detail, new people were to speak to investigators who were already working the assignment. She also mentioned she would determine which investigators had experience in undercover work and would attempt to create a team with experience and training in this area. It was suggested by other investigators to allow only those with this experience to work the detail. Henry believed this should have been considered before the assignment was implemented, without forcing individuals to openly discuss a possible lack of qualifications.

The detail had the marks of a request made by the DA, who passed it on to the chief investigator to be carried out without any planning. This seemed to be the case with many requests for details, and the chief investigator delivered the request without providing knowledge or experience to carry it out.

The day-to-day life of a police officer or an investigator is spent not only performing the job, but also preparing for court. Each task may require written reports that could eventually end up in a courtroom all the way up to the highest levels of the legal system, including the Supreme Court of the United States. If a person loses their credibility to testify to the facts, their profession might end up destroyed. Losing credibility and where that would leave them never seemed to be a consideration for the DA's office. The real question was whether the justice system would ever let such a stumble occur.

The major case homicide division of the office had large numbers of cases where defendants were in custody past the ninety-day limit for indictment. This meant their cases needed to be presented to a grand jury who would decide if the cases would go to trial. During a meeting addressing the issue, the DA blamed attorneys for failing to read the case files to obtain information needed to present to a grand jury. When Henry worked with the attorneys, many of them were overwhelmed with balancing the large volume of cases. The situation could potentially allow a murder defendant the opportunity to be released because they were not given due process.

To a person accused of a serious crime, this could mean the world. How would any individual feel sitting in a jail cell for months, not knowing if their case would even go to trial? After all, an arrest and a person's initial appearance before a judge is, at this point, still only an accusation.

While sitting at his desk one day, Henry overheard his supervisor at the time, Georgio Pitts, attempting to find someone to obtain a DNA swab from an individual volunteering to be tested. He asked Henry if he was comfortable handling the task. Henry asked if there was a search warrant completed by the investigator requesting his assistance. The supervisor ignored Henry's question and explained that the homicide division supervisor in the office was trying to find someone who was comfortable doing it because his staff was too busy. Henry asked if there was a case file or any documents to support his request. There weren't. Based on that, Henry chose to not perform the DNA swab, not feeling comfortable doing it without a search warrant or knowing the details surrounding the need for the request, other than that the person consented.

If the person submitting the DNA sample was later implicated in the crime, they could recant their consent if there was no warrant, claiming the DNA sample was obtained against their will. Under the Fourth Amendment to the Constitution, which governs search and seizure of government entities, the burden of proof is on the entity to show that all searches of people, houses, papers, and personal effects are free of unreasonable searches and seizures. Government entities routinely introduce search and seizure consent forms to be signed by the person consenting to the search. This is a substantial step that shows the search was consented to by the individual. The duty also rests upon the authority collecting a sample through a signed consent which, if challenged during the legal process, would show that the consent was provided freely, without coercion. Why would two directors of divisions attempt to obtain DNA involving a murder case under any circumstances without a search warrant or a signed consent form along with a case file of the facts?

In April 2017, Henry returned to work after two weeks on family medical leave due to the day-to-day stress of the environment. He was quickly reminded of why he needed time off in the first place. When Henry unlocked the door to his office, a box of evidence related to a child sexual assault case sat in his chair. There were no instructions, emails, or notifications to explain why it was left there. This was improper and violated all evidence chain of custody. The case number on the box was relative to a case from 2015. When he looked up the case's activity narrative, he could find no current information displayed as to who worked on the case last or the next steps needed. Henry left his office to see if he could locate a supervisor or someone within the division who might have placed the evidence there. He could find very few investigators in the vicinity that day, including the supervisor, and those Henry asked were not familiar with the evidence. When he returned to his office, the evidence was no longer there. He had received no email or phone call notification that someone had picked it up.

At the beginning of June 2017, all trials and related work were stopped immediately until further notice. After almost two weeks of an apparent shutdown of the courthouse and procedures, Chief Investigator Stoneheart said during a staff meeting that trials would resume, so all investigators were warned to be prepared because, according to Stoneheart, "the judges are going to slap it on us." Henry took this to mean that a large amount of work and responsibility would be placed upon them with little time to prepare. Investigators were also warned that if they were not prepared, it was their fault. Investigators were now expected to be responsible for any shortcomings of cases which resulted from the shutdown. The chief investigator later advised investigators that the stoppage was due to an improper jury process by the county. No clear details were given as to why the jury process was improper, which could have consisted of several issues, such as the actions and behavior of a juror or concerns and conflicts related to the attorney or county government. Regardless of the issue, it impacted the legal process and procedures that affected lives.

During one of the weekly meetings in June, after the trial shutdowns were lifted, Henry met with his assigned prosecutor and the judge to discuss case updates and which cases were expected to be ready for trial. After discussing both Henry's availability and that of the attorney, the judge raised a concern that the DA was delaying things by not having prosecutors available to try cases. The judge concluded there was no obligation to accommodate the state by delaying the defense teams, if they were prepared for trial. As the presiding judge, she expressed that she had to protect the rights and best interests of the accused. The judge's comments sounded valid, as Henry too believed it was equally important to ensure fair justice is provided to the accused, just like the fight for justice for victims and safety of communities. When the judge completed the case assessment, the attorney verbalized that this was a bad position to be placed in, as the delays caused by the trial shutdown also affected the ability to manage and resolve cases while preparing to resolve others. This could also lead the judge to have certain cases dismissed if the office was not prepared at the moment of request.

Toward the end of the month of June, Stoneheart called an emergency meeting to discuss a trial scheduled that day which involved gang members. There were rumors that gang members planned to show a united front during the courtroom proceedings, as well as intimidating potential witnesses and their family members, however there were no actual threats communicated to investigators. Investigators were directed by Stoneheart to request and record state identification from anyone entering the courtroom. If the person did not have a state ID, they were required to provide a phone number or some other form of identification and would be unable to enter the courtroom if they did not meet the demands of the request. The way the solution was approached seemed unconstitutional. The chief was reluctant to explain any details which would confirm that this approach had legal support. Under the First Amendment of the United States Constitution, through the Supreme Court under case study (448 U.S. 555 (1980), the public as well as the press have a right to attend court trials. An attempt was made by the defense attorney in a murder trial to request a closed courtroom after two mistrials. The closure of the court was granted, but then reversed by the Supreme Court in July of 1980, also citing 443 U.S. 368 (1979). It held that the ability to attend trials allows the American justice system to maintain and protect freedom of speech and the press. The process is also said to ensure the public's confidence that criminal proceedings are open for public discussion. In order to deviate from allowing courts to be open to the public and the press, there must be have been overriding and countervailing interest articulated.

Even though the case may have dictated a high level of awareness and security, it was unheard of to request identification to enter an open courtroom or request contact information from someone without identification.

The reason for requiring identification was that gang members were known for not carrying identification in case they were suspected of something if stopped by police. Therefore, if a gang member arrived, they would be declined to enter the courtroom when they could not provide ID. These efforts did not appear well-thought-out but were possibly the personal approach of the chief investigator and the district attorney, who made the decisions of how investigators should carry out their request. Henry's belief was that anyone who approached the checkpoint area could have easily provided false information such as a phone number, an address, or other identifying information. With no ability to verify any of the information, it defeated the purpose of asking for the identification.

In day-to-day encounters with citizens, police officers don't request identification with every encounter or force citizens to present identification without probable cause. No legal reason was provided by Chief Stoneheart as to how her directions gave her the authority to deviate from the law enforcement standard for providing ID or personal information.

The idea to require ID was scrapped before it even took place. No information was given as to who reversed the decision. It was disturbing to know that this requirement for ID had probably taken place in the past. While explaining the procedure, Stoneheart had told investigators to place tables out in front of the courtroom like before. There was no other clarification of what "like before" meant, which could lead anyone to believe it had happened in the past. The chief investigator never provided any legal support behind the requests she routinely asked of investigators. Henry was unsure if she had ever understood the freedom and protection allowed under the Fourth Amendment search and seizure and how this freedom and protection could easily be violated.

In August 2017, Henry attended an investigator staff meeting in which the chief investigator discussed protocols and procedures for obtaining trial evidence. Investigators were now required to use a specific form to obtain cell phone data from defendants, and this would be used to obtain the data just before the case went to trial. A couple of investigators, including Henry, looked around the room in total shock. One investigator asked how the form was expected to be generalized to all defendants without assessing whether the crime was facilitated by using a cellphone or if it even possessed specific evidence believed to relate to a crime. Another investigator even presented an example where a search warrant for phone information was requested by a prosecutor without probable cause. The judge ultimately denied the search warrant, confirming no probable cause to request a search of the cell phone based upon the crime. Henry was aware of many cases that were handled by the office where the agency presenting the case for prosecution had already conducted the proper investigation to show whether a cell phone yielded evidence of the crime, and evidence such as phone records had already been retrieved and preserved as evidence. In other cases, it was determined that the accused had a cellphone in his possession when arrested, however nothing listed the cellphone as evidence in the property or that it had a relationship to the crime. It is not enough to pursue evidence for the convenience of confirming a crime. There must be facts which accompany the belief that the search will yield specific evidence. It is also important to ensure that the agency seeking prosecution is not working against the agency prosecuting the case. When two investigations contradict one another, it also presents concerns over integrity and quality.

Chief Stoneheart explained that she did not want anything illegal done but wanted the investigator to try to find probable cause to search a phone. As an investigator, Henry believed the statement made by the chief investigator was not clear or specific in explaining how the form related to the search of a cell phone, or how far the investigator needed to go to establish incriminating evidence. The form was just one of the criteria that needed to be met in order to search the cell phone for evidence. The other was to establish probable cause to have a judge sign a search warrant, but Stoneheart failed to combine the two and meet both.

Although investigators in the office routinely applied for and requested search warrants to strengthen a case, all law enforcement personnel should be uncomfortable requesting search warrants from a judge without factual probable cause. When investigators presented the concern to Stoneheart of a judge refusing to sign a search warrant, her response was to simply find a judge who would. However, in Henry's experience, it was always frowned upon in the law enforcement profession to "judge shop." This "shopping for a judge" is jargon used in the court environment where law enforcement staff go from judge to judge until they find one who favors a particular statement or testimony and signs the warrant previously denied by other judges. This process can appear as undermining the decision of the judge and the judicial system. Although judges are expected to remain neutral and detached, seeking out certain judges could tempt those requesting the documents to withhold or fabricate information in their favor.

Throughout the inconsistent processes in the office, Henry remained professional and performed his job while assisting other investigators where help was needed. In August 2017, Henry observed a fellow investigator bring several pieces of evidence into his office for trial that would take place over the next few days. Some of the evidence consisted of rifles and shotguns. Henry asked him what his plans were for storing them, because the universal key system used in the office made the evidence accessible to others. The offices were routinely left unlocked for cleaning as well. Since he had no other plans except to leave it in his office, Henry suggested he call the investigator assigned to the office and responsible for storing case evidence for trial and have him take possession, or to return the evidence to the prosecuting police department to have their agency store it. The investigator ignored this advice and chose the typical path for handling evidence in the DA's office, irresponsible as it was. As Henry walked past the office door the next day, he could see the evidence sitting in the same place. This investigator, like many Henry witnessed, engaged in practices that not only compromised cases, but risked jeopardizing their careers.

CHAPTER 7

Who You Are Matters

IT HAS BEEN THE BELIEF IN WORKPLACES, as well as society, that laws, rules, and standards are applied the same for everyone, no matter who you are. However, in the criminal justice system this is a misconception, and is far from reality. Regardless of the best efforts used to process cases, District Attorney Rollins did not appear to have a systematic, consistent approach based upon facts. His decisions on which cases to prosecute or dismiss seemed based on his personal desires rather than a systemic approach based on the defined elements of a crime.

Cases that had the same criminal charges and met the guidelines and elements charged were commonly dismissed from prosecution, while others continued through the process. In 2013, before coming to this office, Henry investigated a sexual assault incident while employed as an investigator for a metropolitan police department. A sexual assault had been reported by one of the local universities and involved a female student and several male students. The university's police department didn't staff members with the training to handle this type of incident. The campus police gave Henry a summary of the details. A student and her mother contacted police after the victim had been at an on-campus party and had possibly consumed drugs combined with alcoholic beverages. The victim awoke the next morning and found herself totally nude inside a male student's dorm room near the location of the party.

During the investigation, Henry spoke with several male and female witnesses who had attended the party. The witnesses confirmed that the victim was drinking heavily and consuming marijuana, combined with the street drug known as "mollies" or "ecstasy." This drug is a methamphetamine, which alters the mood and perception of the user and has similar characteristics to stimulants and hallucinogens. When both marijuana and ecstasy are used together, the body is not only consuming the stimulant ecstasy, but a depressant as well—marijuana. The marijuana provides a relaxed and controlled "come-down" effect from the ecstasy, which causes confusion and memory changes due to the brain's slow recovery from the stimulant ecstasy. The combination of drugs has a history of popularity at parties, raves, and nightclubs. The victim's behavior changed suddenly, witnesses told Henry, and she appeared delusional and unaware of her environment. She couldn't even get her close friends' names right. Other witnesses reported that the victim went into the restroom with at least two different males on two occasions, and sounds came from the restroom indicating sexual activity.

The victim said she couldn't remember the party or any of the events that occurred. The standard medical sexual assault examination consisted of a rape kit used by a trained sexual assault nurse examiner and a toxicology report to assist with the diagnosis of drug influence. The rape kit can provide DNA clues. Even though the DNA clues may assist with identifying individuals, it plays no role in determining whether or not a victim's consent to have sexual intercourse was either given or legal, under the conditions one is able to give consent. Based upon the information described by the witnesses, the victim was believed to be having sexual activity in the restroom after the victim seemed unaware of her surroundings. Witnesses further advised that the victim could not identify many of the people at the party. She had walked around dazed, a disillusioned look on her face, addressing friends and fellow students by the wrong names.

When investigating sexual assaults cases, it is important to determine a victim's ability to give consent to take part in a sexual encounter. Although the victim was conscious during the events, her statement that she could not remember any of the events was a good indicator to aid in demonstrating her vulnerability and inability to make decisions. During the process of speaking to all witnesses, Henry discovered valuable information related to the victim's day-to-day demeanor and personality. Witnesses stated that the victim displayed a "hard to get" personality when interacting with males. If approached in a flirtatious or sexual manner, she would quickly decline their advances. In order to gain clarity on what that meant, Henry followed up by asking if it would be common for the victim to have sexual activities in the bathroom with two male students at different times within that night. The response was that the victim's behavior and actions were out of character and not normal. Henry ultimately pursued criminal arrest warrants for the male students identified as suspects.

This same information was available to District Attorney Rollins when he decided to dismiss the case more than a year later. Henry speculated that the decision not to indict was more than just a legal decision; it was related to personal relationships Rollins had with the university. Henry believed decisions were made to preserve the reputation of the university by not prosecuting or accepting concerns that males attending the institution were sexually assaulting female students. Henry witnessed cases that were prosecuted with far fewer facts and evidence than this campus incident, where even the prosecutor was uncomfortable trying the case.

A sexual assault case in the office could take from one to three years from the time the case was filed to the time the case was resolved. This time would include the initial indictment and any hearings or reset dates of the case, until a disposition was reached.

However, the university case took the same timeframe to determine only whether the defendants should be indicted.

When a criminal case reaches the DA's office, probable cause has usually been met by the arresting officer or investigator. The long delays before trial consist of hearings related to the case or rescheduling the trial to continue preparation. The delays never consist of attempting to determine if the case meets the basic elements to prosecute. When a case is indicted by a grand jury, a prosecuting attorney has already presented the basic information of the case and has suggested that the elements of the crime charged were consistent. Even when Henry sat down with the assigned attorney to discuss the cases, he was told that many of the delays came from the district attorney and his personal decisions about the case, rather than being based on facts. But the ethical standards of how cases were handled consisted of more than the actions of the DA.

On a consistent basis Henry observed a prosecutor abuse a resource that allowed inmate cell phone calls to be monitored and later used as evidence. As a "friend" contact of the prosecutor on the social media site Facebook, Henry noted that she would post the basic contents of the jail conversation online. The comments on the post insulted both the accused person and the person they were communicating with. The prosecutor expressed disbelief at the conversations she recorded. There is no reason anyone could use to justify this disrespect. The attorney's behavior displayed superiority over those who were accused of crimes. Even more disturbing, this attorney was a seasoned professional with many years invested in the system.

Investigators were told numerous stories by Chief Investigator Stoneheart of how this prosecutor had contributed to several successful cases. Maybe these results gave the prosecutor confidence in her ethically questionable behavior. Even the day-to-day policies, such as arriving to work, fluctuated and were unclear.

One of the policies or personal rules of Chief Investigator Stoneheart was that if an investigator was not in the room for her weekly meetings by 8:30 a.m., they needed to wait outside and explain their reason for being late. There were two veteran investigators who were never on time and would enter the meeting only to be addressed with a comical remark by Stoneheart such as "I guess they can start now, since you all are here." This created an environment that fostered negative attitudes rather than cohesiveness, teamwork, and camaraderie. The investigators looked at one another, remembering her previous statements that if you were late, to wait outside to explain why. When the meeting was over, all investigators went to their destinations, and the two that walked into the meeting late never stayed behind to speak to the chief investigator to explain.

In 2015, the DA's office faced a great deal of ridicule after an employee was terminated for sexually harassing a female witness in a case he was assigned. This was one of two incidents with this employee. The first was a murder case where the witness was the ex-girlfriend of the defendant. Many would question how this was allowed to happen—not once, but twice.

During media coverage of the murder case, District Attorney Rollins was subpoenaed to testify and was asked about the behavior and why the employee still had employment after more than one incident of harassing behavior. Rollins's testimony was that he was trying to help the employee rehabilitate himself. After additional information was reported of the trial, a witness testimony confirmed that the accused employee told a witness that he had no concerns about any repercussions because he knew the district attorney had his own issues. It seemed the employee was implying that he had negative information which could affect the DA if he ever tried to punish or discipline him. It also seemed apparent that they were known issues of concern with the employee's behavior, which prompted the DA to use the word "rehabilitate," which is generally used to suggest that someone is trying to be restored to a normal position from that which created the abnormal state. The term "rehabilitate" is also commonly used to communicate that an incarcerated person has reformed and is ready to be released into society. Rehabilitation is also described as someone who has recovered from some form of addiction. Although the office had to carry on with business as usual, this incident created an environment that made Henry embarrassed to be an employee.

There were other incidents in which investigators were allowed to take advantage of the very loose standards in the office. One investigator, after the birth of her baby, began reporting to work nearly every day between 8:50 and 9:00 a.m., sometimes later, rather than 8:30 a.m., which was the expected reporting time. The only instances where she was on time were the Friday morning meetings for investigators, unless that meeting was cancelled. Why was she able to arrive on time for the Friday morning meeting but not the other days? Henry's belief was simply that she was not held to task.

The direct supervisor of his division, Georgio Pitts, was well aware of the different standards. At times this same investigator would lose her composure when dealing with difficult witnesses and victims and would speak out loud in an open setting. Her comments would sometimes be, "Fuck that bitch, she doesn't know who she is messing with" in reference to a witnesses or victims who were hostile or refusing to testify in court. The supervisor would be present and not intervene or redirect the behavior. This was no surprise, as Henry observed the chief investigator verbally express things in the same manner. This gave the impression that unprofessional acts would not be addressed or viewed as a concern. Lack of professionalism in the performance of one's duties not only gives a bad impression of the office to the public, but also lowers their confidence in how cases are processed. This was dreadful and embarrassing to watch, as Henry could only imagine how someone whose life depended on professional services would feel, if they only knew.

Every day at the DA's office brought a new conflict where prosecutors wanted special treatment while violating policies intended for their own protection. Henry's supervisor addressed a complaint from an unidentified source and added that he would email everyone a copy to make sure no one could say they did not understand or were not aware. The complaint covered several instances where prosecutors were going out to appointments to visit witnesses and victims without investigators. Some were doing this after hours or during work hours when the investigator was not present. This was extremely dangerous, as prosecutors could face retaliation by associates and families of the defendants they prosecuted. At times, with domestic violence cases, defendants are still in the home when investigators and attorneys arrive to conduct preparation for hearings or trials. Henry asked the supervisor if the attorneys were taking it upon themselves and not reaching out to the investigator about interviews or visits to crime scenes. The supervisor did not answer the question and said the investigators needed to communicate with the attorney to find out when they needed to go into the field. Henry followed up by stating that going into the field with the attorney was part of the trial preparation process and needed a formal written request for a task that needed completing. After all, you can't participate in something you are not made aware of. This was also a part of the list of requests that generally accompany the checklist of trial preparation. Henry was rudely interrupted by Litia Sampson, who worked in the human trafficking department attached to his division. She said there was no need for the prosecutor to make a written request because she scheduled her attorney's tasks. The supervisor agreed with her and said it could be handled verbally.

Henry had concerns with this practice based on the management history in the office of blaming the investigator when there were flaws or last-minute issues with a case. Henry was simply asking for accountability and documentation. Henry told Sampson that her practices should not speak for the majority. Documentation was also important, because when attorneys felt pressured to explain a negative outcome with cases, the investigator always seemed to bear the brunt of the blame.

At times, DA Rollins would speak with investigators as a group and try to encourage them by saying they were needed to help young prosecutors who had minimal experience. Some prosecutors were very outspoken about Rollins, who would tell them that prosecutors oversee the cases, not investigators. Investigators were never viewed on the same professional level as prosecutors and were only considered part of the team when something was needed. Investigators never received the email or information that the supervisor discussed in the complaint. The investigators in the meeting looked as disturbed as Henry, both when the conversation began and when it ended.

One Friday in December 2016 Stoneheart covered the status of trials for the week. One investigator announced the results of a trial where the crime was very similar to his university sexual assault case that had been dismissed.

A female high school student accused a male student of rape. The incident took place at a party where there was heavy drinking, and the alleged victim remembered only a few details of the events. She was said by some witnesses to be unconscious when the sex occurred, while others witnesses claimed they thought they heard a woman's voice telling the accused to stop. The defendant was convicted and sentenced to twenty years in prison with a minimum of ten years to serve.

The case was initially charged as a misdemeanor case of statutory rape because of the three-year age difference between the victim and the accused but was upgraded to a felony rape case. The definition of statutory rape in this state was that anyone under the age of sixteen could not consent to any sexual activity. By mere definition of the statute, the incident would be treated as a misdemeanor crime based upon age, but the case is elevated to a felony when evidence exists that a degree of force was used, expressed in this case by the victim saying "stop," according to witnesses. As Henry continued to listen to the presentation, he became disturbed that this case was so similar to his college sexual assault case that was dismissed by the district attorney.

The disparities within the office on many days would alternate from the cases themselves to day-to-day administrative issues such as time reporting. Not a week passed without Chief Stoneheart addressing investigators in weekly meetings or through email and pointing out what seemed to be distrust or lack of confidence that employees would do the right thing. One email in particular said that if the time an investigator put on their timesheet was different than when they clocked out electronically, they were stealing. When Henry began working in the office in 2013, employees with the county, including investigators, used only a sign-in roster system to document their attendance. The paper documents were kept in a notebook in each department. They contained the names of all those assigned to the departments, with a section to write in an arrival and end time for the workday. Then, around 2014, employees converted to an electronic time clock system, where they would swipe an ID badge each day to document attendance. Even though the time clock system was now in place, some departments throughout the county were still using both the sign-in sheets and the electronic clock to manage attendance. Chief Stoneheart, however, had different protocols for documenting attendance. Some investigators, such as those who worked the security protection detail for the district attorney, were asked to report directly to the chief, who used only the sign-in roster. Some senior investigators were expected to use both the sign-in roster as well as the electronic time clock, with some seniors signing only the paper roster. Lastly, there were non-senior investigators who were expected to sign the paper roster as well as use the electronic time clock. This inconsistency created total confusion with the investigators as to the important standards of documenting attendance. No positions, assignments, or policies displayed in the job description of the investigators articulated how attendance is documented for different investigators. Although there may have been special assignments or details which made these procedures more manageable for the chief investigator, it gave the appearance of these being immoral, unfair procedures. When investigators discussed their concerns with one another, most did not feel comfortable approaching the chief investigator or the county administration. They also stated it was not worth the cost of being singled out as someone who caused problems. It was never clear why there were so many differences in how attendance was managed. When there is no clarity with issues or concerns, it gives the impression that the issues are beyond being managed, or the leaders are simply in denial of the problem.

During his career, Henry had a supervisor who was a very strong leader. He told Henry that he never forgot—as a leader and manager—that you may not always be able to treat everyone the same, but to make every effort to treat them fairly. It was obvious that the DA's office operated on plain old favoritism.

Chief Stoneheart said many times that working in a DA's office is one hundred percent a team effort. The team consisted of attorneys, investigators, paralegals, and victim advocates. Everyone must get into the trenches to prepare a case for trial. When the outcome of the trial was positive, prosecutors were in the media spotlight and viewed as the office superstars. When the results did not lead to a conviction, there would be answers required from every division involved in the process. However, the praises, rewards, and even instant promotions based upon case results were limited many times to only attorneys.

An example of this took place in mid-March 2017 after Henry spent a week's work on a draining trial. The case was complex but led to a successful conviction. By the end of the week, news coverage showed photos of the prosecutor, the district attorney, and a new attorney-in-training, but not Henry. The highlights of the case were discussed, along with the efforts of the attorney. It was not out of the ordinary for an attorney to be promoted to senior attorney based on one good case, with the investigator on the outside looking in. As a professional, Henry was taught that a team is only as strong as its weakest link. It was also driven into him that good leaders make every effort to include everyone when achieving success, just as when overcoming loss and defeat.

CHAPTER 8

✺

Manipulating the Glass Ceiling

THE PERCEPTION IN THE DISTRICT ATTORNEY'S OFFICE was that women and men were both given the same opportunities to advance. The reality, in Henry's opinion, was that advancement only happened if personalities, opinions, and interests matched those who managed the DA's office. It appeared as though any level of supervision within the office had to conform to the standards of the office, which was ultimately funneled down to the employees. Merriam-Webster online defines "glass ceiling" as "an intangible barrier within the hierarchy of a company that prevents women or members of a minority group from obtaining upper-level positions." When Henry observed the practices in the DA's office, the definition did not fit the practices of the DA toward the chief investigator, as she was immediately placed in the highest level of authority upon the DA's election in office. It appeared he delegated authority to the chief investigator to control the advancement of both men and women, while they both personally decided who was fit for breaking the glass ceiling. Once individual women have broken the glass ceiling, they should fight to ensure others have the opportunity to do the same. Even if they are not female, they should work to prevent any behavior which could lead to discriminatory practices.

Women have faced barriers in many areas and are striving to overcome the glass ceiling by being strong, independent workers. Although the majority of management positions at the DA's office were held by women, Henry often observed the DA attempting to exercise male dominance over women he considered a threat to his beliefs and decisions.

Individuals speaking up and voicing their opinions should be valued in the workplace, but they weren't valued in this office. Henry sat in on several meetings where Rollins made every effort to dominate the conversation. He asked for the opinions of the women in the room, then often cut them short as though they were not deserving of voicing the opinion he just asked them to give. During his discussion of a very important case, he asked specific questions involving the case. When a female attorney responded, he abruptly stopped her before she could even complete her sentence, while shaking his head no. He then looked at Henry and asked him what he thought, but he allowed him to finish his response. It appeared he didn't think Henry had the best opinion; he only wanted to devalue the opinion of the female attorney. It always puzzled Henry why the DA had little confidence in women but continued to advance and promote those who were willing to accept his and the chief's control.

It came across that the DA thought he could treat his employees any way he desired simply because he was the highest authority. Stoneheart was known to say that the DA was not fond of employees who complained. Even when Henry sat down to speak with the DA as part of his hiring process, he asked that if Henry were hired, he would be sure not to complain. Henry responded that he would not, although he did not have a clue at the time why the DA would ask such a thing. As each day of his employment passed, Henry began to understand that the DA's primary goal was a controlling form of management.

An average day in the office consisted of meeting after meeting involving prosecutors, deputy attorneys, the chief investigator, and the district attorney. On one occasion, the chief investigator attempted to convince investigators that they should be honored to work at a DA's office that was the highest paying public office in the state. Her comments served as a reminder that due to some salaries in the office being higher than other agencies, they should accept whatever treatment or behavior the DA or the chief presented. When employees attempted to meet the DA's demands, they were ultimately held responsible if the outcome was negative. The desire to please the DA seemed to outweigh the performance level of staff members. Even when prosecutors attempted to make the best decisions on cases, they faced the obstacle of convincing the district attorney of their decisions, while fearing he would never agree and would reject their decisions. The attorneys would eventually return to their offices with rejected looks, while discussing new efforts to resolve their cases.

On many days Henry witnessed DA Rollins interacting with leaders in the office, and the atmosphere was fearful and uncomfortable. These leaders were predominantly women, including the chief investigator, the deputy director of crimes involving women and children, the general trial division director, the chief of staff, the human resource coordinator deputy, the public integrity deputy director, the staff personnel recruitment deputy, and the office manager.

Henry volunteered to accompany a prosecutor when she needed to speak with the DA about a complex case. They were a team, and he felt he could help answer questions about the large amount of investigative work that he completed. The attorney declined his offer, adding that she would be okay, and that the DA did not like it when "we" show up. Henry was not sure if she was referring to his race, gender, or position as an investigator. Regardless, it certainly made him believe there was some concern or fear that his presence would interrupt the DA's normal routine of decision-making. It was also disturbing that this attorney obviously had some ongoing knowledge of how the DA felt about others being in the company of the attorneys. It would seem that if the cases were considered a team effort, everyone who worked with the case could provide helpful insight to make the case better or to create a subjective environment. Under the management of DA Rollins, Henry believed it would forever be a challenge for women to break the glass ceiling by overcoming the barrier and still be respected. Even though Rollins promoted women in leadership and other positions, he also appeared intimidating. Henry did not observe this demeanor toward males. True support of those breaking the glass ceiling allows females who are leaders and decisionmakers to perform their duties freely, without being intimidated or negatively influenced.

Although the district attorney expressed at times that certain female prosecutors were very talented, his actions and trust in them did not match his words. Many, including Henry, felt confused and misguided about the criteria for being a leader in the DA's office. Determining your responsibilities and striving to fulfill them did not seem to be valued. Henry observed many attorneys with high standards face resistance and be made to perform as the DA desired, even if it was substandard.

No individual, whether male or female, will accept and understand your worth more than you. A place of employment is similar to a relationship, because it is that. You spend as much time, if not more, interacting with people at work as you do with your significant others and family. If you would not allow a dominant person to affect your family and personal life, why would you yield completely to that in your career? Words like "inequity" and "discrimination" should be joined by "manipulating the glass ceiling." If breaking the glass ceiling requires accepting control and intimidation with no consideration for your opinions, the stage will be set for gender inequality and discrimination. Although a promotion or advancement could be a positive event for a female, it can come with the cost of accepting behavior from superiors which would not be done to males in the same position. This concern should include any treatment that differs from that done to others, or from the expected norm for fair treatment when pursuing or sustaining advancement.

In June 2018 Henry viewed a local news story that said history was being made. The story spoke of making strides and accomplishments with the creation of a new city within the county. The entire criminal justice system where the new city was formed was being led and operated by black women and was the most progressive in the nation. Was it truly a coincidence that the only interested and qualified individuals leading the criminal justice system in the new city happened to all be women, or was it planned that way? Even though these history-making events appeared to be acts of breaking the glass ceiling, Henry believed balance should be maintained in those who form the criminal justice system. They should not only ensure that the best-qualified persons lead our justice system, but also make every effort to be sure a balanced core makes up the criminal justice leaders and employees. There should be a diverse system that includes race and gender. This diverse system should be prepared for and should serve the public—a system that includes citizens, victims, witnesses, and defendants, all promoting fairness. When this is not present, it allows an environment to exist that is susceptible to multiple forms of discrimination.

Henry strongly believed that Lady Justice, who, with balanced scales, represents the image of criminal justice, was never truly given a blindfold. She simply possessed an adjustable one that fit particular standards based upon individual situations.

CHAPTER 9

The Revelation

WHEN HENRY BEGAN HIS EMPLOYMENT with the district attorney's office, he was bright-eyed and ready to take his nineteen-year career to another level. His first goal was to establish good working relationships with those he was assigned to work with and those he was sure to meet. Little did Henry know there would be stipulations to executing those goals.

Henry was assigned to the general trial division around September 2013. He introduced himself to an administrative employee and express how excited he was to be there. Later, four employees, two women and two men, told him to be careful talking with this employee. They explained that certain people were off limits for conversation, and she was one of them. Henry asked who would be concerned with him speaking with this particular employee and was informed that it would be District Attorney Rollins. Henry did not inquire any further as to what his conscience was believing. He also did not want to compromise the new job he had just started by making inquiries about the DA. This was one of many incidents Henry encountered where subtle comments were made that involved the DA having concerns about men speaking to certain female employees.

When Henry had conversations with veteran investigators in the office about advancing his career, he was met with jokes. Some investigators said his sharp and professional appearance would hinder his goals to land advancement opportunities in the DA's office. Henry found this troublesome, as no one ever gave specifics as to what this meant. Reluctant to ask detailed questions as to how this could influence advancement, Henry didn't want to believe his career could be affected based upon the DA's personal beliefs. Little did he know this would be the foundation for the struggles and resentment Henry would face while employed at the DA's office.

This was obviously a problem, and one Henry was not willing to engage by changing his standards or the way he presented himself. Each morning he selected his attire, pressed the seams, and tied Windsor knots. He often wondered why he spent so much effort in an environment where tactical pants and blue jeans were the preferred attire. His quest for excellence did not begin there and would continue on regardless of what anyone else did or thought. The excellence Henry pursued was who he was, but the inability to succeed in an environment with lower professional standards was always frustrating. Every individual can find something they could improve on in their performance, but how can you let yourself regress or lower your standards?

The environment at the DA's office appeared one where not only personal appearance needed the stamp of approval, but also beliefs and character. As an investigator, Henry believed each opportunity for contact with anyone involved in a case had an effect on it. Professionalism played a part in how each witness or victim perceived the office's interest in the case. Nothing will change about first impressions. Henry's personal appearance displayed how he felt about this job. Every day he went out in the field with a prosecutor, individuals questioned which one of them was the attorney. This confirmed what Henry believed—he was appreciated and valued by the citizens. After all, the whole point was to gain the confidence of those Henry represented and served.

A great outer appearance does not always reflect how well someone does their job, just as those who are unhappy are unmotivated to do their job. However, Henry believed that if the district attorney and chief investigator did not like who you were as a person, this would affect your advancement in a negative way. Once employees began to understand this, especially new employees, they made every effort to conform. When in Rome, right? Maybe they had things in common, such as the belief that a lack of valued experience could be compensated with a happy smile. For many years our society's definition of greatness has eroded in some respects. Almost everything in our society today involves a set of rules, regulations, policies, and best practices to achieve maximum performance. It seemed the DA's office selectively decided which standards were accepted and valued. Employers and companies will always own the right to establish their own set of rules, cultures, and standards for doing business. However, when those standards fail to extend fairness and promote positive growth for the company and for individuals, the leaders are operating for personal gain.

CHAPTER 10

His Gender, His Curse

ON A MID-SEPTEMBER DAY IN 2013, Henry relinquished his role as a police detective in the Special Victim's Sexual Assault Unit at his former police department and sprinted toward his new assignment as a prosecuting investigator. Little did he know this would be the beginning of his career nightmare.

Having had a variety of investigative experiences, Henry was certain he would have a successful career that would end at this office. However, in June 2016, the dream of this successful career disappeared before his eyes. Henry experienced what he believed, without a doubt, was sexual discrimination. He tried to apply for a position within the DA's office as an investigator handling human trafficking cases. He was extremely qualified based upon his previous experience. Instead, the position was given to Litia Sampson, who had less experience and tenure than Henry. From the time the position was established in this office, the human trafficking investigator position had been occupied only by women. Sampson would be the fourth woman named to it.

Sampson previously worked as a probation officer and supervisor at a southern metropolitan agency. As a supervisor, she was responsible for overseeing people released from incarceration to a probational status, with the completion of their sentence being monitored by the probation staff members. Sampson then worked as an investigator for a different DA's office in the same region. She moved to the DA's office where Henry worked and was assigned to his division. Although a probation officer is part of the criminal justice system, the position required only a general certification that did not allow the employee to enforce laws or make arrests. Sampson was required only to obtain the minimum certification as a peace officer to get a job in the DA's office, which did not require any previous work as a law enforcement officer. Conversations occurred between other investigators in the division, including Henry, of Sampson starting her career off in the sexual assault division with no prior experience or expertise. New investigators were always introduced during staff meetings, and their prior experience highlighted. In most situations, investigators are asked to start in the general trial division as an investigator before going into specialized divisions, unless they had previous or specialized experience. The term "specialized" did not mean every person assigned to a division had more advanced training or experience than other investigators, it simply defined the difference in working all other felony cases except sexual assaults and homicides. Although Henry did have advanced training in investigating sexual assaults, he had to start as a general investigator. This concerned him from day one, since he was told by the chief investigator in his interview that he was being considered to work sexual assault cases. This was one of the unwritten policies which allowed the standards to be applied differently based upon the personal wishes of the district attorney, or the chief investigator to whom he gave his stamp of approval.

Henry had a conversation with one investigator, Dennis Jenkinsburg, who told him Chief Stoneheart called him to her office and asked him which person should get the position Henry was interested in. When Jenkinsburg became an investigator at the DA's office, he supervised other investigators in both the general trial division and a specialized division, later stepping down to work as general investigator with no supervisory duties. Jenkinsburg gave his opinion to Chief Stoneheart that Henry should get the job, if she was going by experience. He also told Stoneheart he knew she probably had someone else in mind for the position but did not mention who.

Jenkinsburg was very familiar with the needs of and demands on a human trafficking investigator, since he once supervised the division until he was replaced by a woman. Shortly after Litia began working in the office, the supervisor who replaced Jenkinsburg spoke to Henry regarding an incident involving Litia. She expressed her attempt to discipline Litia after discovering that the woman sat in on a trial during her work shift that was unrelated to her duties and responsibilities and which could have caused a legal conflict. The potential conflict was that Litia knew the defense attorney personally who was defending a client that the office was prosecuting. No explanation was given by the supervisor as to why the chief investigator imposed no discipline, even though the supervisor stated it had been suggested. Henry believed it was important for leaders to consistently assess the performance of employees to ensure that their actions and behavior are not compromising to investigations or the justice system. It is also important for the prosecutor to ensure that there are no actions which could create conflict in processing cases. Because Litia worked for the prosecution with direct access to information and procedures of the office, it could have been perceived that she provided an advantage to this individual with whom she was personally involved. Even though it would be the responsibility of the office to confirm the conflict, Henry believed there should also be a responsibility to implement and enforce policies to discourage it.

Managing the disciplinary process is a very important part of both a supervisor's and leader's job. When the discipline process is managed fairly, it affects things such as promotion, advancement, or termination of a person's employment. It can also create division between employees if one employee is disciplined for an incident and others are not, leading to an environment of favoritism. After the opening was announced, Henry sent an email requesting a meeting with Chief Stoneheart to voice his concerns as to why his emails were not responded to regarding his interest in the open position and why there was no formal process. During this one-on-one meeting, Stoneheart told him it was just not his job to have, that some jobs are not for him, and a woman would be better for this position. She then made matters worse by saying, "Some days are just not your day." Hearing that brought a knot to his throat, and Henry became physically sick to his stomach, stunned that the chief investigator and highest-ranking law enforcement officer in the DA's office would say such a thing.

After taking several days to process this, Henry decided to reach out to a civil rights attorney. His trust in Stoneheart to do the right thing had been destroyed long before this, based upon her lack of fairness in managing the office.

Henry sent emails to Chief Stoneheart to express his interest in the position and to District Attorney Rollins to discuss the position. All the emails were ignored, along with any efforts Henry made to express interest. He was never considered for the position and there was no promotion process. Because of this, he chose to record audio of the June meeting where Henry requested to speak to Stoneheart concerning how the selection was made for the open position. He also wanted to support the assertion that Stoneheart, along with Rollins, created and operated an environment that was discriminatory and prejudicial. Under the laws of the state it is legal to audio record a conversation as long as you are a party to the conversation.

After speaking with a civil rights attorney, Henry and his attorney, Roland Spenser Duvall, prepared to file a discrimination complaint against Stoneheart and Rollins. Duvall's firm was based in the Southeast region of the United States, although he practiced in several states. Duvall has been named a "Super Lawyer," one who is recognized as competent in over seventy specific legal subject areas. Super Lawyers must be nominated by peers, then go through peer evaluation and research. Duvall also had a passionate assistant attorney, Conner Drew McIntosh, who he designated as the lead attorney for Henry's discrimination claim.

Once this claim was filed and served to Stoneheart, she announced that any investigator interested in the position already filled by Sampson should send her a resume and apply for the position. Everyone in the room looked around in confusion, because Sampson had already started working in the position.

As a result of this request for resumes, in early August 2016, an email was sent by Rollins's office manager at the time, Rita Cantrell, who worked as an administrative assistant in his office before transitioning to her current position. She left after a few years for a job at another DA's office in the state. Cantrell posted an open position and job title that was named differently than the job given by Stoneheart to Sampson in June, which never had any job announcement or hiring process. The posted position had the same responsibilities and duties as the previous posting but used the word "required" for the minimal education, which was a bachelor's degree. This new job posting seemed to be tailored to disqualify Henry based upon education, which they knew he had not obtained yet, even while he met or exceeded every other qualification. There was no consideration for education combined with experience listed in the qualifications, which was not the case for previous investigator positions.

The job posting was merely a defense, and it was later declared invalid, according to a representative in the personnel department. The DA's office was not aware that Henry had attained all the job descriptions and requirements for every investigator position in the office. Henry spoke to the representative of the personnel department who said efforts were being made to get the job position and title approved, but she wasn't sure that would be successful. When his attorney team became aware of this attempted coverup, the attorney filed a second complaint, citing retaliation for the original discrimination complaint.

In September 2016 the office conducted what Henry believed was one last attempt to cover their tracks. They gave Henry an interview for the new position, although nothing had changed with his educational status. He still had not obtained a college degree from the time the job was posted to when he received the interview notice. The interview panel consisted of DA Rollins and a prosecutor, Lorita Lasalle, the prosecutor who was working with Sampson at that time in the human trafficking division, with Sampson being the investigator. Lasalle had served in the DA's office as an assistant attorney before moving up to a senior attorney position and directing a sexual assault unit within his division before assuming the human trafficking duties.

Nothing in the interview seemed legitimate. The questions were very basic, given his experience. When Henry attempted to answer a question, Rollins cut him off before he could finish. His answers appeared to be of no concern, and his presence simply part of their attempt to defend the discrimination claim. After the interview was completed, Henry received no follow-up response. Discrimination and being overlooked for a position carry many effects that cannot be changed by punishment, either through policy change or monetarily. Being passed over for the human trafficking investigator position stripped Henry of the training, knowledge, and experience that would accompany such an opportunity and gave that to an individual who was underqualified. The position would be great for a career, so being passed over also deprived Henry of advancement opportunities. It gave him the feeling that he, as a male employee, was below standard.

Henry never asked for any special favors while employed at the DA's office. He wanted only to be treated fairly with the opportunity to advance his career based on merit and hard work. Even in the midst of the challenges Henry faced, he was still able to do and be everything he needed to be for his family. Even on his bad days, Henry would not allow his young son to believe that the father he held in high regard was defeated. Henry fought each day to complete his college degree, one of the hurdles the DA's office placed when they discriminated against him.

Regardless of any shortcoming an individual may have, he or she has no control over the actions of another. When destiny is controlled by an outside force, a person must overcome. Whether man or woman, whatever color or creed, no one should be subject to discrimination. They must never rest in bringing to justice those responsible for discriminatory acts. As it is with laws in our country, ignorance of the law is no excuse. As convicted offenders have criminal histories, so should those who discriminate. A citizen has the responsibility to stop and assess his or her actions, and so should those who discriminate. If this burden is placed upon citizens, why should it not be placed upon companies, government leaders, and officials? In every workplace in the United States, posters and signs are plastered in hallways and offices stating the policies and laws against discrimination.

If this system does not work for everyone, it does not work. Most people in society don't ask for or expect special treatment, but they are willing to take action when their rights are violated. Henry believes society needs to understand how one can experience discrimination in an environment such as a DA's office, which should be a place that understands and respects the human and civil rights of all.

CHAPTER 11

Identity of Discrimination

DISCRIMINATION IS A MAJOR PROBLEM because of the many ways it can occur and is believed to have occurred by the affected persons. We all form prejudices within our daily lives; however, when these prejudices become discriminatory, they cross the line. Under the federal laws of discrimination, Title VII of the Civil Rights Acts of 1964, it is illegal to discriminate against an employee based upon race, color, religion, sex, and national origin. It also protects individuals who assert their rights from retaliation. There are postings in certain areas of company and government agency buildings which highlight the federal laws of discrimination. Each year, law enforcement agencies require a mandatory number of training hours to remain certified. This state's mandated officer training requires a minimum of at least twenty hours of training to maintain certifications (Rule 464-5—Annual Training Requirements). The rule establishes that a minimum of five of the required twenty hours of annual training consist of the following topics:

- Firearms requalification—1 hour
- Use of deadly force—1 hour
- De-escalation training—1 hour

- Community policing—2 hours

There is no mention of required hours in areas such as discrimination. However, many criminal justice issues in society raise concerns of criminal justice practices and how fair justice is applied. Not all acts of discrimination are intentional; some may be due to lack of training and personal experience. There are no direct pre-employment screenings which define whether a person has discriminatory tendencies or prejudices against others. However, it is just as important to bring awareness each year to professions such as the criminal justice system, where lives have the potential to be negatively impacted by discriminatory practices. Failure to assess these issues and learn how to prevent them sends messages that the behavior is only a problem after it has been alleged. Government agencies tend to detour from mandated training on discrimination because they refuse to acknowledge it exists; doing so would create liabilities which could later result in someone being a victim, and they usually are. When discriminatory government agencies are challenged it may also force disciplinary actions in addition to costly, ongoing civil litigations. Constant training and awareness can provide clear expectations of the desire to prevent discrimination. It then becomes a personal choice of those who discriminate, rather than agencies and companies allowing discriminatory acts to occur. Addressing individual violators of discrimination early is easier than compromising the positive reputation you wish to have.

When a government agency acquires a reputation of having discrimination issues, every function within that environment becomes questionable. These are the very same functions the agency depends on—fair hiring practices, promotions, and treating victims, witnesses, and defendants fairly as part of our criminal justice system.

In early December 2016, the Friday morning meetings resumed after they were stopped for the Thanksgiving holiday. The drama and the presentation in these meetings were consistent with that of a dictatorship, having a controlling feel to them. The meetings included all investigators, with Chief Stoneheart stating how things would change in the coming year. She informed the team that there would no longer be any tolerance for family issues such as lack of a babysitter or marital stress due to working long hours. Like most of her conversations, Stoneheart used a harsh and disrespectful tone, as though she were disciplining children. Some investigators, including Henry, expressed that this demeanor was intimidating. She summed up that if they could not accept the changes, they needed to consider whether the job was right for them. Although Henry understood the change, as did other investigators, he believed the chief should have asked if there were other ways to handle her concerns. This would allow discussions to determine whether valid concerns involving an investigator's family needed additional attention and consideration.

Stoneheart attempted to be positive by reading a letter of thanks from a citizen to Investigator Sampson for work done on a case. After reading it, she added that Sampson's patience in dealing with a female victim after hours was the reason she was given the position of human trafficking investigator. This situation was the focus of Henry's discrimination complaint. Although Sampson was only doing her job like everyone else, Stoneheart highlighted all Sampson's positive actions.

Stoneheart's justification for giving Sampson the job shifted frequently. On this particular day, she was singled out for her patience and the way she worked with the case mentioned. In the discrimination complaint, when Stoneheart explained why she gave Sampson the position, she said only that she needed a female for the position because women are better but said nothing related to their performance or experience. Neither did she give an explanation of what they were better at, just that they were better. What truly concerned him about Stoneheart was that she was still making no changes in her behavior or the way she led in the DA's office, even after having her discriminatory actions and other issues brought to her attention. She seemed unaware she was facing discrimination and retaliation claims.

Many times, confusion exists over what our civil rights are, how to stand up for them, and how to protect them. These rights include many areas of the justice system. When violated, these rights are also violating federal laws. These laws protect all United States citizens against issues such as excessive force by law enforcement, illegal searches and seizures, miscarriage of justice, and discrimination. Title VII of the Civil Rights Act of 1964, as well as the Fourteenth Amendment, state that every citizen has the rights to life, liberty, and property, without due process of law.

The reality was that Henry's DA's office created an environment where civil rights and equal rights were nothing but words. Employees and citizens who encountered the office may have easily found themselves chasing human and civil rights forever, without success. Individuals may always encounter incidents they believe to be discrimination and unfair treatment. The challenge will be having someone come forward with an effort to hold the violators responsible. Even as the DA's office and criminal justice agencies advance and promote employees, some will have opportunities that lead to success and others will not be afforded the same fair opportunities.

The professional environment seems to have struggled with identifying and eliminating employees whose personal beliefs interfere with business operations. Henry believed Chief Stoneheart and District Attorney Rollins allowed their personal beliefs to decide what was fair with employee management. Workplace discrimination may start with an individual, but it ends in a much bigger problem if the organization or company knows and does not address or prevent the issues going forward.

In January 2017, Chief Stoneheart presented work schedules for a mandatory high-profile assignment. Volunteers were requested to fill hours for the assignment. After only a few moments, Stoneheart became angry by the lack of interest by investigators for certain shifts and assignments. She stated that investigators agreed to their duties when they took the job. She also reminded everyone that they had been informed at the end of the previous year to take care of anything that might interfere with working the assignment with an understanding that different assignment hours would be needed to complete the task. However, when investigators were asked to volunteer, due to low morale within the office, no one showed any enthusiasm to volunteer, but they also understood that the ultimate goal was to provide justice to victims. After observing the chief's anger, individuals did pick shifts needed to complete the assignment.

The stern speeches were nothing new, nor were the requests for volunteers to work special assignments. Stoneheart continued her discriminatory practices by suggesting that men work the 12:00 p.m. to 8:00 a.m. shift. She added that she was not being racist or anything, but "some of these ladies have babies." She then stated that if she needed to fill in for any women, she would, because that is what family does. Although the chief was attempting to clarify how important it was to have the assignment hours covered, she was being sexiest, suggesting male employees accept certain hours as opposed to females. This was another example of her personal beliefs allowing her to discriminate against others with work assignments. The chief seemed to be trying to show that she was not discriminating, because the assignments did not target a race—but they did imply gender.

She stated that her request for men to take certain shifts because some of the women had babies was not policy and ended by saying that if someone wanted to write her up to go ahead, and she would admit she said it. Henry felt she was attempting to exercise authority and power over the room. As the highest authority in the office, there would be no one to report her actions to other than District Attorney Rollins. Henry could not speak for the rest, but based on his previous experiences, Henry had no confidence that this unfair request would be treated with any concern. He also believed Chief Stoneheart felt comfortable saying whatever she wanted because she had the support of the district attorney. Henry saw this problem as bigger than her and should be owned by District Attorney Rollins and the entire county government.

Even though his civil action against the DA's office covered specific incidents, Henry felt discriminated against every day he showed up to work. Records confirmed that Henry was the one investigator whose knowledge, experience, and job tenure—although greater than 75 percent of the investigators—didn't warrant a single promotion. Henry transitioned from the position of general investigator into the specialized division working sexual assault crimes. This transition did not come with any pay increase or fringe benefits. Henry seemed to be viewed as a necessary evil, only to be called upon when it benefited the office or no one else was available.

In June 2017 Henry reviewed the contents of his legal case, which contained a response from the county stating he was not discriminated against but was instead unqualified. As Henry read, he became disgusted all over again with the lies, deception, and unethical acts committed when those involved are clearly wrong and their deeds discovered. The county claimed Henry did not appear to be interested in the position, even though his formal request through email notices went unanswered. The county's response also highlighted that Henry did not have desired responses to the interview questions; he was not familiar with and up to par with computer skills needed to perform the job; and finally, the person given the position had a five-year plan for the position. Henry found it sad but humorous that they continued their attempts to justify it. Nowhere in the employment world do you begin working a position and then interview for it months after starting. The best way to determine the qualifications would've been to review the state's certification database which contained officer training files. Perhaps this never occurred because it was never the objective to find a qualified person. The district attorney's office liked to use a phrase in closing arguments of criminal cases that said, "When you can't argue the truth, then you just argue." This situation was just like that phrase.

When you team ignorance with control and power, you face a vicious enemy. Each day Henry's thoughts about his discrimination case failed to provide an understanding of how one can experience discrimination in an environment such as a DA's office, which should protect and respect the human and civil rights of all. Justice is best served to those who encounter the criminal justice system when the best candidates are selected for all positions. When society faces crimes such as human trafficking, where children are preyed upon and other victims are sexually assaulted, the DA's office has a duty to protect them and provide justice with the most qualified person for the job. When government agencies and organizations discriminate in deciding who defends and protects us against predators, they have not only failed the victims, but they have failed society.

❋

CHAPTER 12

Defense by Retaliation

ONCE BOTH FEDERAL COMPLAINTS WERE SERVED against Chief Investigator Stoneheart and District Attorney Rollins, ongoing incidents tested Henry's patience and endurance.

In September 2016, Henry worked mandatory detail that began at 5:00 p.m. and was not completed until 9:30 p.m., after a full workday. Prior to beginning, his supervisor, Georgio Pitts, told Henry that he did not need to return to work to clock out if he worked under the time clock system. Henry could simply leave the detail and drive home, but he was required to report his hours the next day to Stoneheart.

Pitts always needed prior approval from Stoneheart before making many of the day-to-day decisions. Henry did use the time clock to document his work hours for the previous evening, as instructed by Pitts, but his paycheck stub for that time period did not show any hours for the detail that he worked. Henry emailed Stoneheart and inquired about the missing hours, although he was not expecting a response based on her history of ignoring his emails. Surprisingly, she did respond, asking Henry if he clocked out after completing the assigned detail. Henry explained what Pitts instructed him to do. She responded that she did not ask for that information. Henry was confused but patient in asking her what she needed him to do next.

Stoneheart said Henry could only get compensatory time since Henry had not clocked out, which meant Henry could take the time off at a later date. This was not an issue, but it shows the inconsistency in the office. Or was it intentional, meant to deny Henry the ability to receive the documented hours as he was told?

Stoneheart would often deviate from her own instructions regarding overtime. Some days overtime pay would be provided to investigators as an option. Other days, investigators were advised they could not receive overtime hours, because working late was sometimes part of their job responsibilities. Henry eventually requested to leave early in exchange for the time he had worked the assigned detail. When he emailed his supervisor, he was advised to get approval from Chief Stoneheart. Henry felt tossed back and forth when he tried to get authorization from his supervisor and the chief investigator. Many days he requested things from his supervisor and would be told to see the chief investigator. Other times Henry presented a request to the chief, she would tell him to see his supervisor. It was always frustrating. Henry felt the government agency should have had some type of intervention preventing Stoneheart from managing his career, knowing he was involved in a discrimination claim against her.

In October 2016, Henry submitted a time-off request for the upcoming holiday season to spend time with his family. Once Henry submitted his request, he was approached by his supervisor who said, "You will be tired of seeing Santa Claus after taking two weeks off work. Are you going out of town?" Henry had not yet determined his plans and asked his supervisor why he asked. The supervisor responded that Stoneheart might want to see a copy of his travel arrangements or some kind of verification. Henry told him she could speak with him, if needed. Henry did not understand how his plans mattered in order for him to have his vacation request approved. Nothing about the request was outside of policy, and documentation to confirm travel was not required.

A continuous game of chess seemed to be playing out, with the county hoping that someday Henry would grow frustrated and just lay down his king. However, Henry refused to give in until there was accountability and justice. He would soon have a Christmas vacation and wanted to use part of that as preparation for a less stressful new year. He only wished his vacation could have come sooner.

One particular Monday morning after Henry clocked in, he received a call from his twelve-year-old son telling him he had missed the school bus. Henry informed his supervisor that he had an emergency and needed to leave. Henry's division normally had a Monday morning meeting, so this meant Henry would be absent. After taking his son to school, Henry received a call from his supervisor asking if he was headed back to the office. Henry told him that he could head back and asked if he needed something. The supervisor explained that Stoneheart asked about his presence during the meeting, although this was only a division meeting headed by the supervisor that the chief investigator never attended. Henry's supervisor asked him if he clocked out to go to his emergency. Henry hadn't, as it was not a general practice to clock out unless they were leaving for the day, just as they would not clock out for a lunch break.

Henry sent an email to both Stoneheart and his supervisor asking if he needed to submit a leave request to cover any time missed. He simply did not want any hassle about why he needed to go. He received no response to the email. His supervisor later called and said it was not necessary to fill out any paperwork, but that Henry should have contacted him when his time away was done. Henry apologized for not informing him but did not understand the need to, unless there was an assignment that needed completion. Previously, his supervisor would let him know the day before if he had any tasks for him to complete, or he'd simply call him on the phone. There was never any requirement to check in or inform him or the chief when going from one place to another, even when it involved the cases they were working on. It was normal for investigators to come in to work and see and talk to the supervisor for only ten minutes and have no further contact the rest of the day. This was apparently not the case this day. When Henry inquired if the supervisor needed anything when they spoke, he responded that he did not need anything, but the chief was asking where Henry was and that he should call him to find out. This too was uncommon. Even when investigators were absent for meetings, supervisors did not call them to see where they were, unless a work-related request was needing to be completed. Henry had made no attempts to be treated differently by advising his supervisor that he was leaving to take his son to school after missing his bus. Henry arrived to work on time but wanted to make his supervisor aware of where he would be. As an investigator, the workday commonly consisted of driving to several metropolitan areas to conduct investigations, so they were not confined to any specific area. They were also not required to clock out for breaks or lunch; therefore, it was also common for investigators to run errands during that allotted time. Henry believed that if something happened while he was completing any task other than work, that he would have been punished, so Henry asked before leaving to attend to his son.

Henry felt this was an effort to keep total control over his day-to-day activities in the office, with the hope that he would do something to devalue his character. Henry spent as much time attempting to figure out how to defend their next attack as he did in performing his job.

In early January 2017, his division was instructed to meet with Stoneheart to discuss the agenda for the upcoming year. During the meeting she asked each investigator if they were getting along with their assigned prosecutor. When the question got to Henry, he responded that things were going okay. Stoneheart said she'd heard from other prosecutors that things were not okay, and Henry was refusing to do tasks as requested. Although quite upset that he had been confronted in front of the other investigators, he was familiar with Stoneheart's lack of professionalism. She turned to his supervisor and asked if any concerns had been brought to his attention. His supervisor said that the prosecutor did not have concerns with his performance, and Henry always seemed to be focused on the task at hand.

If there had been concerns with the performance of his duties, a meeting should have been called in a more appropriate forum with the person who had the issue rather than calling him out on it publicly. When the meeting ended, Henry asked to speak with both Stoneheart and his supervisor in private. He displayed his concern with how the incident was addressed in front of other investigators rather than privately. Henry felt proper measures should have been taken to confirm that the information was valid. Henry's supervisor said that the prosecutor in question had expressed concern over times she needed to go places to work on cases, but Henry had not been available to take her.

Henry explained that a few issues had arisen between the prosecutor and himself when he was asked to subpoena out-of-state witnesses to attend hearings without the proper paperwork to legally complete the task. The second issue was when the prosecutor insisted on having evidence brought to the office against the policies and protocols set forth by the DA's office. Henry closed his thoughts by advising that the prosecutor never requested to be taken anywhere to complete case work. Both Chief Stoneheart and Supervisor Pitts appeared dumbfounded and did not have much to say but responded that they understood.

In staff meetings with all investigators, Stoneheart would tell investigators that she expected experienced investigators to help prosecutors who may not have much experience. Henry always believed he was assisting the prosecutor by reintegrating the legal concerns with providing subpoenas and processing witnesses who live out of state while at the same time processing evidence, both of which could affect the outcome of cases. Henry believed this applied to everyone except him. It was obvious that this incident concerned coworkers who respected him. One investigator told Henry that the chief was wrong in her approach and that he had handled the situation professionally. It was reassuring that through all the adversity, staying professional had prevailed overall.

The first few months of 2017 were extremely challenging for Henry. He had a complex trial in March with many witnesses who were uncooperative and refused to appear in court. While navigating these obstacles, Henry had to work more than fifteen hours one day to finish locating individuals for trial. During this long day, Henry developed a massive migraine. Even after going home and attempting to medicate, Henry could get no relief. He laid in bed the entire day on Saturday, trying to find relief and to recuperate from the previous day.

Henry still couldn't shake the migraine on Sunday, so his wife drove him to an urgent care center. Before going, Henry took his work-issued cell off the charger, making sure there were no other issues with witnesses needed for the trial, including one witness coming from out of state. Henry had emails and text messages telling him that he needed to report by 9:00 a.m. on Saturday, which he missed because of the migraine. After seeing the missed messages, Henry received a call from Stoneheart, but he had stepped away from the phone and didn't answer in time. When Henry attempted to call back, she did not answer.

On Monday Henry was approached by Stoneheart who asked him in a loud, aggressive voice why he did not answer his phone over the weekend. Henry explained that he was sick over the weekend, but she appeared to have no concern about his well-being, but only why he didn't answer the phone. Henry asked whether it was mandatory that he answer his phone at all times, even though he was not on call and was not a supervisor where he would be expected to answer.

"No, but if you have a big case, you need to check it!" she yelled.

She also questioned why Henry did not leave a message when he called her back. Henry ignored her question since he had already explained being sick. He didn't understand why, if it were so important, *she* had not left a message after her initial call. The task she was referring to had already been completed by another supervisor in the division. Stoneheart jumped on the opportunity to chastise Henry, nonetheless. She also requested Henry send her a memo explaining why he did not answer the phone or come in.

Several investigators never responded to emails, phone calls, or text messages even while working their scheduled hours.

Feeling he was losing a battle with stress, Henry made an appointment to see his therapist in March 2017 for guidance, which the urgent care staff had suggested. The therapist recommended Henry take medical leave from work to deal with the stress. Henry was given medical orders to separate from work for a couple of weeks.

When Henry gave the orders to the office manager, he was told he would be receiving paperwork for processing and approval. When Henry attempted to reach his immediate supervisor Martha Kittle with the information, she was out of the office. Kittle was fairly new in her role as supervisor as well as at the office, as she had been employed there less than one year.

He sent an email to let her know that he would leave a copy under her door explaining his request for time off. She asked why Henry had just informed her today, so he explained that he was given the orders that day during his appointment. Her response felt bitter and unwelcome. She said Henry should have informed her of the appointment.

Henry's initial thought was to give up his position to relieve himself of an environment with no hope for peace or fairness. However, Henry refused to yield to an environment that ruled by control and fear. He made a decision to accept no more of the attacks against him. After getting the cold shoulder when he submitted his medical paperwork, he was ordered via email to attend a meeting the same day, within two hours. He was sure it would be related to his medical leave document, so he immediately notified the legal team handling his discrimination case that he was at the end of his ability to tolerate attacks and acts of disrespect and was now being asked to meet with his supervisor and Chief Stoneheart. Henry was instructed by his attorney to request the meeting be rescheduled so they could attend.

With the discrimination and retaliation case pending against Stoneheart, neither his attorney nor Henry felt it would be a good idea to meet. Stoneheart denied the request to reschedule and said the meeting would go forward with or without his legal team present. Henry alerted his attorney of her response, and they informed him to attend the meeting, if only to hear what they said.

When Henry arrived, there appeared to be a major shift in attitude and demeanor by Kittle and Stoneheart. They talked about clearing the air with his issues and concerns at the DA's office. Henry was told not to take things personally or let decisions at the office affect him. It appeared they were attempting to relieve the tension. However, Henry didn't understand how individuals who discriminated, isolated, and disrespected him would expect him to not take things personally. Nothing was said during the meeting to give him the impression that things would ever change. Henry made no comments and dismissed himself when Stoneheart was finished.

Each day became a struggle for Henry to get dressed to come to work and to avoid conflicts. However, when Henry looked past the negative encounters with Stoneheart and offered to meet the professional needs of the office, he was again rejected.

During a meeting in June 2017, Stoneheart announced an investigator was leaving the juvenile courts and would be replaced by an investigator who had worked in the office for around five months. In the past, selections for that position had been based on a proven track record of handling very demanding assignments. Henry volunteered to transition into the position in 2016 after the office was unable to recruit anyone. He completed a letter of intent and applied, but nothing happened. When Henry followed up, he was told by the chief investigator that she would check on the status, and this too never happened. These acts, even after a year, were not only deceptive, but led Henry to believe that the primary goal of the chief investigator, district attorney, and those who represented them was to punish him and make his employment extremely uncomfortable.

CHAPTER 13

Words are Powerful

AT TIMES, THE ENVIRONMENT in the district attorney's office became a scene of turning select employees into victims of ridicule, embarrassment, and disrespect by Chief Investigator Stoneheart. During several of the weekly investigator meetings, an investigator would be targeted, laughed at by a room full of other investigators, and made to feel worthless by Stoneheart. She typically treated the investigator as though he were a child. She asked pointed questions, attempting to highlight how the investigator was not doing his job. Henry never observed her belittle any of the female investigators in the meeting. This investigator never seemed comfortable in performing his duties, and Henry believed Stoneheart took advantage of the fact that he was nonconfrontational. He never said anything that was insubordinate or disrespectful to Stoneheart to warrant her behavior toward him; he only attempted to defend himself by telling Stoneheart he was not really trained in certain areas being critiqued. Although the job duties she targeted were his responsibility, the tone and attitude of the chief investigator was completely inappropriate.

She would call some investigators liars and challenge them publicly if there was something she did not agree with. At times, she would address issues in general, then refer to the incident and call the investigator lazy and trifling. Stoneheart made it known that if investigators didn't meet her standard of approval, then she and the DA's office did not need them.

During one meeting she claimed Henry's division was weak and needed to improve at pressuring victims and witnesses to comply. Many investigators didn't want to tell her if they had a problem locating individuals for court out of fear she would get on the phone and make the situation worse by cursing the victim or intimidating them with arrest. She also regularly called out supervisors, telling them to be tougher and do a better job supervising.

During a personal meeting with Chief Stoneheart in June 2016, which Henry requested, she said he had an attitude and said his "ass was on his shoulder," later stating that Henry was walking around looking unhappy. Henry didn't walk around with a smile on his face, and it wasn't a requirement, so he didn't know why this was an issue. She never addressed any issues with his job performance, but she did add that Henry should not expect a leadership role with that attitude.

This convinced him that not only his career path, but that of others, depended upon how Stoneheart felt about an employee's personality rather than their performance. If investigators fell short of a goal, the fear of reaching out outweighed the fear of negative results. Leading by fear was the foundation of her managerial skills.

Near the end of the June meeting, she mentioned that she once worried what people said when she became chief investigator. That changed, she said, when she started doing what she needed to do to get respect. When she did, her career took off and she never looked back. She stated she had not asked to be chief investigator, but District Attorney Rollins had given her the job anyway. She added that he showed some hesitation, because he knew as well as she did that she did not hold back on speaking her mind.

This appeared to be the crux of her problems—an inability to consider the feelings of others. Even her emails were sometimes full of anger. The comments were in red and all-caps, leading the recipients to believe there was some resentment on her part. At times the emails displayed total ignorance, eventually forcing Stoneheart to muzzle herself and not respond at all.

One investigator decided to retire based on the low morale in the DA's office and Stoneheart's conduct. She explained she'd had to address the chief investigator on more than one occasion for not treating her like a professional. During the week that this investigator was leaving, there were no announcements of her retirement or any events to honor her. In the past, Stoneheart had at least made an announcement and appointed another investigator to handle a celebration.

When this investigator's last day approached, another investigator told Henry that this employee did not want anyone to make a fuss over her. Regardless, Henry and two other investigators decided to do something for her. They went to the store, purchased a cake, and presented it to her. She was in tears and grateful to be acknowledged, as anyone would have been.

In November 2016 Henry had to locate a former police officer for an upcoming trial. While talking with her, she mentioned she had applied for a position as a criminal investigator for the district attorney's office Henry worked for. She had worked three years as a police officer and had taken several classes to become an investigator but decided to pursue a path to become a criminal attorney. She did not confirm whether she completed the study but said she had decided she did not like it. She received an interview in his office but was told by Chief Investigator Stoneheart she did not have enough investigative experience. The officer felt she was qualified based on education and years as a police officer as described in the job posting.

It was not in Henry's character to discourage someone from pursuing a job. Henry advised her to not question her abilities but expressed that her strong personality and inability to be influenced probably worked against her in this environment. After all, why would she be disqualified when others were hired directly into specialized units with equal or less experience? Henry also wondered if this woman's wish to rise higher exceeded the standards of an office whose morals seemed stagnant.

In November 2016 Henry's older sister, who lived in another state, passed away. Henry contacted his supervisor to make him aware. The supervisor did not express much concern and would only discuss how he felt receiving the same news about his own family member. The supervisor said he understood if Henry wanted to keep the matter private, but he needed to make Stoneheart aware to have his leave time authorized. Henry never received an offer of help or was asked if he needed anything.

Traditionally, leaders and employees would send out condolences via email, phone calls, or in person. In some cases, they would collect donations for assistance. During Henry's career in the DA's office, he had a few deaths in his family where neither Rollins, Stoneheart, nor his supervisor bothered to express concern or condolences. Even though it was extremely painful to work in this environment, it was what Henry had come to expect from a place where he saw little moral integrity.

Each week his division had a Monday meeting, and Henry took his regular position holding up the wall. This was his regular spot since he was never comfortable taking a seat in an environment where he did not feel welcome. During one meeting Henry looked down at his phone and noticed a work email. It was a reminder from Stoneheart concerning the death of an investigator's father that occurred at the same time Henry lost his sister. She offered condolences, a reminder that donations were being collected, and a request for all to sign a sympathy card. Henry dropped his head. He could not imagine that a leader could be so thoughtless as to not extend respect for any employee's loss. There was no doubt she knew, since Henry had to make her aware.

When Henry returned home for the evening, he checked his email for the last time to ensure he didn't miss any important messages. Henry viewed another condolence sent by Stoneheart, but this one was about DA Rollins. His mother-in-law had passed away.

There was also a request from the family for donations in lieu of flowers.

Not a week passed where investigators weren't reminded of their shortcomings. In January 2017, during a meeting with the chief investigator for his division, Stoneheart spent less than a minute speaking about the good job the division had done during 2016. The remainder of the fifteen- to twenty-minute meeting covered only the shortcomings. She explained that investigators needed to be forthcoming about completing tasks for cases, especially when locating individuals for court and having them appear. There would be times when not every person could be located, she told investigators, but if they continued to say they had successful leads that did not produce results, they will have done the victims a disservice.

In early February 2017, Henry's office set off on a blame game after refusing to pay an out-of-state law enforcement official's expenses to come testify. During a trial in February 2017, the professional witness, who was a police officer, arrived to testify and explained that he had been guaranteed by the trial attorney that all expenses would be reimbursed. After the county refused to pay the two hundred dollars for travel and missed wages, the witness demanded to speak with those involved in making travel decisions.

Henry received an unprofessional email from Stoneheart which read, "Why were you not in control of your witness with transportation to and from hotel and court?" He did not immediately respond to the email because he wanted to be careful in his response to avoid any accusations that he was disrespectful or unprofessional. As he was contemplating how to respond to the email, he received a call from Stoneheart to come to her office, so he did not respond to her original email. Henry also did not want an email response to be taken out of context. The misunderstanding about expenses was between the witness and the prosecutor.

When Henry arrived, he was asked the same question that was in the email. He explained that he completed the necessary tasks to accommodate the witness. The problem the witness had was not about transportation, but rather his missed time from work. Stoneheart was not pleased that Henry had done his job according to policy, nor did she trust what he told her, so she asked for the witness's phone number. She called the witness and said the office did not pay for missed time from work and suggested he contact his state legislature about increasing the witness fees which are offered to testify out of state.

In June 2017 Stoneheart gave a mandatory training session to all investigators assigned to the office. During the training she emphasized several subjects. The first was in regard to work hours, which she said, as she had many times in the past, were from 8:30 a.m. to 5:00 p.m. If anyone needed to leave early, they were to notify either a supervisor or her. She spoke about the honesty of those who signed the paper timesheet in addition to using the electronic time clock. When the subject came up about documenting attendance, Henry felt it was an ongoing issue in which Stoneheart personally chose selective enforcement rather than standard enforcement. When there are no standards, it sends a message that there is known dishonestly in the office, but no aggressive action to discipline those responsible. If there were concerns of individual integrity, they should have been addressed by other means.

CHAPTER 14

My Way or the Highway

AS A MATURE, PROFESSIONAL EMPLOYEE, Henry never knew that "do as I say, not as I do" was acceptable in the workplace. This was the case daily in the district attorney's office for DA Rollins and Chief Investigator Stoneheart. Investigators were constantly reminded to be professional while processing cases and working with other agencies, businesses, citizens, victims, and witnesses. However, both the chief investigator and Rollins consistently deviated from these expectations.

Any attempt to get an agenda across to the staff in the DA's office consisted of a long speech by Stoneheart about changes and being open to them. Change seemed to happen only when it was in Rollins's and Stoneheart's best interests, while both presented change as though it was in the best interest of the office. When changes occurred with investigator assignments, Stoneheart did not select the best investigator to fit assignment changes, but only chose as she wanted. It was always best for an investigator to agree with what Stoneheart wanted rather than challenge her or voice opinions. When challenged, Stoneheart took it personally and would then manage that employee based on her personal likes and beliefs rather than professional management standards.

Most vacant positions that were specialized, such as homicide or sexual assault, were filled by new investigators who were unaware of the lack of organization in the office. These positions required a higher level of investigative experience and were believed to be paid at a higher salary. Neither of these criteria were completely true. The investigators hired, past and present, always discussed the struggle to get a higher salary, if they could get one at all. Not only did they have no choice as a new investigator, they were without a voice and did not appear comfortable expressing their opinions.

Investigators with little or no experience could have a serious impact on trials for homicide and sexual assaults, with the greatest impact on victims and families. These investigators also faced a huge amount of stress.

Henry became close with one investigator who shared similar struggles. This employee had tried with tremendous effort to get into the public integrity unit but was passed over three times without any explanation. Like Henry, he never understood why other investigators would be promoted to senior investigator or other positions when they lacked experience and seniority. One day his coworker revealed that advancements or promotions were contingent on whether an employee had an outgoing personality or was liked by the chief investigator and the DA.

The investigator told him he asked his supervisor why he was not considered for promotions. He was shocked when told he wasn't sociable enough and that he had the demeanor of being upset or unapproachable. His coworker's next question to his supervisor concerned him as much as it did Henry. He asked if he was doing his job successfully, and the supervisor responded that he was. Regardless of his performance, it appeared his career, like Henry's, would never peak, and his worth was based solely on what others thought of him. This was not only disheartening, but the supervisor's response was a carbon copy of the attitude of the DA and the chief investigator.

Not only did they seem comfortable expressing that the employment practices were unfair, but there was a vibe that one must accept the behavior or leave their career. If his personality had been like Henry's, his outcome for success would likely be no different. They both had only one mission coming to work—to do the best job possible. However, it appeared they were faulted for not having a personality that matched "the norm," or one that would make those in charge feel comfortable with their actions. Henry truly believed that the injustice of being unrecognized for your performance was equally as bad as being treated unfairly and punished for your differences.

On occasion, county employees were asked to fill out surveys about working for the county government and to voice any concerns about their work environment. The surveys at the end of October 2016 seemed to serve no purpose because no changes were ever made. Many suspected Rollins and Stoneheart only wanted to assess the climate of the office to know which concerns they needed to get out in front of for liability purposes instead of dealing with the issues. Each year seemed to bring equal or greater employee distrust and lack of enthusiasm. More and more employees raised their heads, squared their shoulders, and took a path toward peace of mind. Employees continued to resign and escape the intimidating "my way or the highway" environment created by Rollins.

The enemy in any battle, mental or physical, gains momentum if their opponent loses focus or surrenders. It is the ones who refuse to surrender that the enemy fears. Henry has learned to not focus strictly on what can be seen on the surface of people and to not fear it, but rather to concentrate on finding out what they don't show or what can't be easily seen. We all have faced or will eventually face the worst in people, but we must closely identify and address those behaviors which are overwhelming, intimidating, and discriminatory.

From the time Henry started his career in the DA's office, he saw many lives impacted by the tremendous stress of working under Rollins and Stoneheart. Lives and personalities changed as they gave in to the domination and control. During his twenty-three-year career in the criminal justice system, Henry never felt even a fraction of the stress or lack of support as he did in the DA's office.

One day Henry had the opportunity to read an online law enforcement article about post-traumatic stress disorder (PTSD), also referred to as complex PTSD. It explained how law enforcement officers who faced unknowns all day tended to suffer more trauma in their careers than military personnel in some war situations. According to Mayo Clinic's website, PTSD is defined as "...a mental health condition triggered by a terrifying event—either experiencing it or witnessing it. Symptoms may include flashbacks, nightmares, and severe anxiety, as well as uncontrollable thoughts about the event." Henry began to wonder if this diagnosis had shifted into his lane. The environment in the DA's office gave him constant feelings of anxiety and stress. Henry was in fight-or-flight mode whenever approached by any individual within the DA's office. He became unsure who to trust in the workplace; he constantly wondered if he could meet even the smallest expectations of the office and feared he would be forced to resign. At this point, there was no way Henry could seek similar employment while gracefully separating from the DA's office.

He was unsure whether other investigators had begun to observe and relate to the struggles he faced by experiencing them firsthand. Henry had two separate encounters with different investigators who expressed concerns about the state of the office and other issues. One investigator asked why his division selected a new supervisor with less than one year of tenure. Henry could only conclude that the chief investigator and the DA liked their personality.

Another investigator said she was experiencing heavy resistance from her supervisor and the chief investigator. The issues started after she was informed at the last minute on a Friday that she had to work on Saturday related to a case. Since an investigator's normal work schedule operated Monday through Friday, this was a concern for the investigator, since it was a last-minute request. As the investigator expressed her concern, she stated that Chief Stoneheart was inconsiderate and unprofessional by not explaining the requirements for working an extra day to allow preparation and become familiar with case information and her involvement. When the investigator arrived on Saturday, she was told the day's focus would be on cases that needed immediate attention. Instead, they spent an entire four hours eating food, laughing, and discussing only one case. This was extremely upsetting to the investigator.

The following Monday, she was called into a meeting by her supervisor and two deputy attorneys in her division. They told her they had observed her appearance and outward expressions in the past Saturday meeting and that it seemed she was not happy being there. She explained she was unhappy coming in for an unproductive Saturday to eat and socialize. The investigator said the supervisor told her that DA Rollins was aware of the incident and was not pleased with her attitude and that her job was at risk because of it.

According to her, it did not end there. She was later called into a meeting by Stoneheart, who questioned whether the investigator really wanted to work there. Stoneheart suggested she apologize to the DA for her attitude during the weekend meeting. The investigator thought her career there was over simply because she expressed dissatisfaction with using her day off for an unproductive day at work. The supervisor then began examining every task she completed to make sure it was done to perfection.

In mid-March 2017, Henry received a phone call from a former coworker at a metropolitan police department. The officer asked Henry to speak with a second officer who was considering taking a job in the DA's office as an investigator. The first officer explained to the second officer that Henry would be a good person to ask because he was honest.

Henry had to be cautious in voicing his full concerns. He was not at liberty to discuss any details related to his discrimination complaint. Therefore, he would be unable to freely give his opinion of the office if asked. When the officer spoke with him, she expressed a couple of things that concerned her. The interview she participated in at the DA's office did not cover expectations of the job but focused more on personality. In addition, during her interview with Rollins, he expressed his dislike for those who complain, and said that if someone didn't like the job, they should just find another one.

The officer asked if there were any complaints going on in the office and how they were being handled. Henry told her there was absolutely nothing being done about them but avoided giving any details. It was again obvious that the office had no desire to change for the better. Either it was their way or no way. The interview seemed to be designed to determine if and how long someone would be able to tolerate the behavior at the DA's office. This was why Henry's discrimination complaint was not about him, but rather about being a voice to promote overall change in the criminal justice system.

CHAPTER 15

🌼

Occupational Oppression

MANY EMPLOYEES AT HENRY'S district attorney's office could have taken a stand against work practices and standards that were unfair if they had accepted that they were in captivity. Just like the history of slavery and the trailblazer Harriett Tubman, many could have been freed.

Employees in the DA's office had the opportunity to go elsewhere, but many believed they had limited options based upon their own strengths. It's easier said than done to pick up and move to a new place of employment or to a whole new career. Employees may attempt to assess the personal skills they have to offer another employer, while some have invested many years and feel they can't compete with a younger workforce. DA Rollins and Chief Stoneheart created an environment that lacked clear instructions and expectations, which caused a stressful and fearful work environment.

Besides the day-to-day demands, employees have the pressure of feeding their families. Regardless of what negative things occurred in the office, employees might feel they have limited choices for survival if they were to become unemployed. Henry had countless conversations with coworkers who expressed their desire to leave a job they were good at and liked in order to escape the controlling, unfair, and overbearing environment. They believed they were victims of unfair treatment but were afraid to exercise their rights. They had a wide range of concerns, including favoritism, discrimination, harassment, hostile work environment, and retaliation. When Henry asked some of them why they did not come forward, many of them simply asked what would be done about it if they did. The DA seem to have as much consideration for his employees as he did for those he was eager to prosecute.

In August 2013 Henry had a conversation with a former investigator who was aware that he had accepted a position at the DA's office, and he warned Henry he was making a huge mistake. He was familiar with Henry's work ethics based upon previous cases assigned to him that Henry investigated as a police detective. He then stated accepting the job would be a mistake because he knew of Henry's belief that fairness should always be practiced by those who represent the justice system. He added that his previous success would never play a factor or be valued, and that Henry would only occupy a position, nothing more. He expressed that Henry's success would ultimately rest on how Rollins and Stoneheart felt about him.

Like many would be, Henry ignored the warning. He was excited about the opportunity, and as he settled into his new role, he spoke with another former investigator who had worked at the office. She expressed that the tremendous stress of the job was causing her health to decline. Her doctor was concerned with her blood pressure and suggested she change her career immediately before it affected her health. She followed the advice and resigned. At a follow-up visit, her physician found that her blood pressure was normal and no other health concerns were present.

Henry heard more stories like this, but he refused to allow the information to discourage him from the new path he was pursuing. The longer Henry worked there, the more he discovered that the environment was intimidating to anyone who chose to challenge issues of operational and policy concerns and fairness toward career advancement. Henry would see many coworkers in a depressive state after visiting with Rollins or Stoneheart, either in a group or as individuals. Their demeanors reminded him of a child returning in tears after a scolding by a school principal.

In October 2016, two more employees joined the list of resignations. One of these investigators made a powerful statement: "If you see the ship sinking, you need to jump." Rollins told the employees that this investigator's services and good work would be missed by the office. Rollins also joked, "I think you may need to sign a confidentiality statement before you leave." Others in the room laughed along with him.

Henry considered ending his employment at different times, but he felt it would only allow the office to win. He wasn't going to turn over a job helping victims, because he enjoyed the work and was proud of it. Encouraging employees of high character to leave ultimately punishes the crime victims, who should be the primary concern.

No attempts were made to address the high turnover rates or the damage that occurred by not having enough qualified employees to effectively process cases for trial. The shortage of attorneys and investigators led to overwhelming caseloads and continuances requested due to not being prepared for trial, both of which contributed to the outcomes of trials.

Henry had the opportunity to assist an investigator who was struggling with the decision to continue employment. The investigator felt bullied by the assigned attorney after the misunderstanding of a comment made by the investigator regarding culture. The incident was considered resolved by the office, and the comment determined to have been taken out of context. This investigator feared continuing to work because the incident could cause her to be treated differently by others. The investigator didn't feel comfortable going to Chief Stoneheart out of fear of not being supported. She explained that Stoneheart asked many times prior why the investigator even wanted the job any longer. It was very common for investigators to have issues within the office, but they would communicate them only to one another out of fear that

Stoneheart would not support them or consider their concerns, and they did not want to be "the problem."

Henry put aside his duties that day to assist the investigator with processing a case due for trial. Although Henry had not been in the exact situation, he could relate to the feelings of being in that environment and feeling isolated. The investigator also shared an incident with Henry about a longtime friend who was a former employee of the office. Henry was shown a text message where the former employee stated that she loved the job and would have continued her career there if not for Rollins. The message summarized the feeling of being bullied and intimidated by Rollins.

After hearing so many stories, Henry felt a sense of responsibility to those who didn't have a voice of their own. Henry believed employees simply did not understand or have the energy to address a work environment that was unfair, hostile, or discriminatory. The DA's office was a right-to-work employer, which meant that an employer had the right to terminate your employment at any time. Although many investigators were aware there needed to be other articulable reasons to terminate employment, this still deterred employees, especially when reminded by Stoneheart that they worked at the liberty of DA Rollins. Some employees feared to exercise their constitutional rights, those rights that supersede the "right to work" practices if rights are violated.

Workplace oppression can sometimes be the hardest to identify. Just like beauty being in the eye of the beholder, oppression is in the eye of the oppressed. There are many instances when an individual experiences issues they feel are unfair in the workplace, but they make no attempts to address them. This could cause them to feel depressed and oppressed without any clear path to a resolution. The most important step is to address internal feelings first. If you don't feel you are treated properly, there may be valid concerns. The next step is to ask if you really want to take a stand and address the issue or quietly leave your career environment for other opportunities. These decisions can only be made by the individual.

Most Americans dream about advancing in their jobs, not regressing. The DA's office standard was to operate with a quid pro quo system and always seemed to lose the trust and confidence of seasoned employees.

In December 2016 Stoneheart reached out to investigators in their first year of employment and requested they meet with Rollins but didn't mention the reason for the request. Other senior investigators learned of this only after speaking with those asked to attend. Henry believed this was an effort to boost morale or to check the pulse of the office. DA Rollins discussed ways he could make things better within the office, including establishing a vehicle assignment program that had failed in the past, but when proposals were brought forth nothing was ever done and some of the attendees reported they did not feel the DA was ever sincerely interested in making things better. Perhaps it didn't matter what the seasoned investigators thought because the office had already lost their respect.

In February 2017 the DA attempted to take a substantial step toward addressing years of employee neglect. A ceremony was set up to recognize some employees who were promoted, and others who had not yet taken the oath required by their positions at the DA's office. This was not a normal occurrence. In the past, an employee who was promoted would simply begin the job without a ceremony. There was still no relief for other employees who were working diligently without deserved promotions.

For many years a huge emphasis was placed on "if you see something, say something." Normally this was geared toward possible criminal activity, which society deemed an extremely important issue. Throughout history, many civil rights leaders had the ability to spark action by promoting morals and addressing individual civil rights. In today's world, it seems society is concerned only with national and public rights violations. It becomes extremely difficult when environments such as the DA's office operate by creating fear to discourage making other issues public. Henry believed those aware of rights violations must act, even anonymously, to promote change. Henry used to believe that addressing violations of individual rights did not require national or special attention. However, if they choose to not let their voices and concerns be heard in some way, they allow an unprofessional work environment to exist that is capable of violating civil rights.

CHAPTER 16

Set the Captives Free

MANY EMPLOYEES WERE ABLE TO LEAVE the district attorney's office by resigning gracefully and thanking the office for the opportunity. However, in private they expressed happiness to be relieved of the torture. This was very common. Attorneys and investigators left to work for other district attorneys, law enforcement agencies, or private law practices. From January 2012 to 2018, 326 employees resigned their positions in the DA's office.

Most employees in the office remained professional, even in times of frustration. Careers in the justice system come with the belief that when major concerns are attached to a criminal justice agency, it reflects upon the whole system. Therefore, employees silently leave their criminal justice careers—to protect the reputation of the profession and avoid jeopardizing their career by opposing concerns.

On some occasions, employees chose to resign their positions and were told by District Attorney Rollins that their timing was unprofessional. Henry witnessed this while using computer resources available to investigators to access forms and other work-related documents needed to perform daily tasks. There were all types of letters available for viewing by any investigator who accessed work-related forms. These letters were not sealed as part of an employee's work or disciplinary file, such as with personnel files or Human Resources. The letters included disciplinary items, welcome letters for new hires, and salary increase requests. How did these letters, which were disciplinary in nature, become intermingled with forms and drafts used every day for both investigator and attorney work resources? In Henry's previous experience, this information could only be seen in an employee's personal file. An attorney's role in the justice system is very important, such as preparing cases to meet court deadlines. However, if an attorney or any employee chose to end their employment, the process should involve a professional separation in which one informs the office and the office accepts the separation and reassigns outstanding tasks or cases. The primary goal should not appear personal but should ensure that responsibilities are delegated. It is considered a courtesy to give as much notice as possible when leaving, but it is not a requirement. It seemed DA Rollins attempted to discredit the attorney as a professional rather than accept the separation.

New investigators were sometimes discouraged from interacting with veteran investigators. Henry didn't know whose idea that was, but it was interesting to see new investigators reach out to other new investigators for guidance rather than to those who had valuable experience. A couple of the new investigators approached Henry after being told to steer clear of him and that he was trouble, with no mention of the source. This concerned them because not many of the new investigators seemed comfortable in their roles, and they thought avoiding veteran investigators was immature. This also explained why inexperienced investigators were directed by supervisors to handle training new investigators.

When an investigator wanted a change of pace, such as a different position or job within the DA's office, it was never acceptable to approach either a supervisor or the chief investigator. If an employee did approach either, they were told their current role was what Rollins wanted, even if their experience could prove beneficial elsewhere. Chief Stoneheart felt the need to periodically remind investigators that it was not about them. Henry wondered many times if any employees understood where they would be best suited to benefit crime victims. Was it about the victims at all or was it about pleasing the district attorney's office-management beliefs? There were no career paths given to employees explaining how to pursue other goals within the office or the county. Henry had never had a job during his career where supervisors refused to outline the steps to a better position until he started at this DA's office.

Henry made several attempts to apply for positions within the county related to his job, such as worker's compensation investigator and investigator in the county solicitor's office. He was hoping for a change from the chaotic environment of the DA's office. He was confident that he was well-qualified, but he never received any interviews, calls, or inquiries about his interest. Instead, Henry received form emails stating that he did not meet the qualifications. Some positions would open, then close an hour later. Henry believed they more than likely had a person in mind for the position already but opened it just long enough to say they made it available to everyone. Henry spoke with an employee who said he wanted to take a position with less responsibility to alleviate his stress and maintain a stable family life. DA Rollins stated there was only one position in the office available, which would be *his* position if he was unhappy being there. The investigator ceased efforts to inquire about other positions because of Rollins's comment. In Henry's opinion, this implied that the investigator would not have a job at all if he insisted on pursuing another position against the wishes of Rollins.

Henry had another conversation with an employee who confirmed that the demands of the office and the DA led to their divorce. Rollins's demands had become overbearing and an obstacle in the marriage because it made a work/life balance impossible. Henry always tried to give encouraging words to anyone he encountered who had concerns in the office and with their career decisions. Henry advised him that a work/life balance was important to consider and he should make the best decision for his overall life.

It was difficult for Henry to communicate with employees and recommend they stand up for what they believed, especially after it appeared some of the discussions may have made their way back to leaders. During general investigator meetings, Chief Stoneheart would make subtle comments that investigators should be aware of who they followed and how they were influenced. Whenever asked, Henry continued to voice his opinion of what he believed was the right thing to do. He never made any efforts to sway new investigators from their beliefs or to share his experiences but would suggest to those who approached him with problems or concerns about their job that they should address supervisors about it properly and professionally.

In early January 2017 Henry returned to work from a much-needed mental break from the constant flow of unpredictable events at the office. After his return, a staff meeting took place with Chief Stoneheart regarding events for the upcoming year and also touched on some from the end of 2016. Investigators were told that another supervisor had chosen to leave the DA's office for one in a smaller county. This was the supervisor who had wanted to step down previously by taking an investigator position with no supervision but was deterred by Rollins. Investigators were also told that the DA's office manager submitted a resignation after occupying the position for just over one year, but there was no explanation of why. Since the position was part of the administration department and not one that worked closely with investigators, the investigators were unaware of information about what drove the resignation. The last resignation announced was an experienced victim's advocate. Henry spoke to her just before the holidays, and she shared her dissatisfaction with being overworked and underappreciated, with a greater emphasis on being underappreciated; her passion for her job was never about the pay.

In early February 2017 the hits kept coming as the office suffered another loss of experience and manpower. A supervisor retired after becoming eligible based upon the vesting period required by the county and accepted an investigator position with a smaller district attorney's office. This was the second supervisor in less than three months to abandon their position for one as an investigator with no supervisory duties or benefits. Although this could be seen a step backward by many, relief and peace likely followed the environment of chaos and high turnover.

As a leader, there is much to be understood about the difference between imposing fear upon people and earning respect. Fear drives resentment, retreat, and radical behavior. Many of those Henry spoke with before resigning expressed their fear of being terminated or never being considered for advancement if they voiced their concerns. Some said they believed nothing could be done if an elected official or those he designated punished them for addressing concerns or standing up for their constitutional rights. Henry never had a conversation with anyone who resigned who still maintained respect for Rollins and Stoneheart's leadership. Henry believes respect promotes growth, teamwork, commitment, and pride while providing an inclusive atmosphere. If there were ever a question as to which atmosphere an individual or institution is leaning toward, one has only to look around to see who is drawn to them and who is running away.

CHAPTER 17

※

Much Bigger
Than the Office

THE COUNTY HAD A SLEEPING DRAGON of issues even before
Henry's employment began, including sexual harassment claims,
unethical payments for IT work, and litigation over improper
overtime management of first responders. There was also a resolved
lawsuit for failure to pay assistant district attorneys a salary
comparable to solicitor attorneys for the county. The taxpayers are
forced to foot the bill for these immoral and unethical incidents.

When the county chose to start a new system to manage
attendance, it introduced a new wave of unfair practices in several
departments. Choosing to go to a time-clock system meant certain
employees had to arrive promptly in the morning. Previously, the
county had a liberal policy of allowing employees to arrive between
certain hours and still be considered on time. Although Henry was
not aware of any formal policy, it was the practice employees were
known to work under, both before he arrived and during his tenure.

A flexible start time was helpful because it allowed for the
unpredictable traffic that routinely occurred in the busy
metropolitan area. Many employees would arrive at the county's bus

shuttle site in time to catch the ride and arrive at their offices on time. However, poor management of the shuttle system and unpredictable schedules resulted in people arriving late, and this added to their stress. Employees reported the concerns to the county personnel department as well as the transportation company, but the situation did not change.

Investigators were informed of the changes involving the time-clock system by Chief Investigator Stoneheart and told that there was no allowance to make up any time if they were late. If late, the time was deducted from total hours worked at the end of the pay period even if the cause was unavoidable, such as a late shuttle. There was also the chance of disciplinary action.

Employees would sometimes wait thirty to forty-five minutes for a county courthouse shuttle to transport them from the personal vehicle parking lot to the Superior Courthouse. Many times, employees became frustrated with the wait and began walking, out of fear they'd face disciplinary action or have time deducted from their paychecks. According to Google Maps, the route was 3.6 miles, or twelve minutes if driving in light traffic. However, rush hour traffic in the busy city was never light. In 2017, the parking was sold, and a new location became the parking area to catch the shuttle. This location was seven-tenths of a mile from the courthouse. For those who walked, a summer day in a humid southern climate, even at eight o'clock in the morning, would have them arriving at work drenched in sweat and forced to work that way for the day. It was never considered that some employees might not be medically fit to walk any distance or were unable to pay a deck parking fee for a closer spot. The waiting list to park closer appeared to be filled based on favoritism rather than from a list or a first-come, first-serve basis.

The DA's office operated between the hours of 9:00 a.m. and 5:00 p.m. Most court services were not provided until 9:00 a.m., with some operations not available until later. It would seem reasonable for positions such as that of investigator to allow flexible hours, especially when investigators were told on several occasions by Chief Stoneheart that they worked until the job was complete, with no defined hours. Some positions could be stopped at 5:00 p.m., while others could not be confined to a specific time.

Henry's position, like other investigators, consisted of trying to reach victims and witnesses whose schedules did not always match the hours of the DA's office. Several requests had been made by investigators to the chief investigator to remove the strict times, but with no successful outcome. An investigator's duties consisted heavily of going out in the field to meet witnesses and victims, which required undefined hours. Their duties and hours were based upon the case research. The DA's office and the county did not appear to have much concern whether employees would perceive the environment to be fair, even if the policies and procedures were legal.

The problems within the county government went much deeper than the DA's office. During a staff meeting in December 2016, Stoneheart expressed appreciation to investigators for assisting one of the courtrooms during a trial. The county sheriff's department, whose duties included managing the courtrooms as uniformed deputies, had a manpower issue was very thankful, because they were struggling to keep up and were knocking on wood that there would be no incidents.

Henry found it disturbing that investigators were needed to serve as plainclothes backup if something happened in the courtroom. There was no joint standard training between investigators in the DA's and sheriff's offices to manage courtroom protocols.

In 2005, a defendant attacked a sheriff's deputy in a courtroom. He changed his clothing to blend in with the public and went on a shooting spree in the courthouse. The defendant ultimately escaped wearing civilian clothing, which would be no different than the attire worn by an investigator. If investigators were placed in the courtroom due to a shortage of sheriff staff during this tragedy, they could be tasked with moving specific individuals to safety, such as judges, jurors, attorneys, victims, and even defendants.

Henry had the opportunity to speak with a deputy in 2016 who spoke about going up for a supervisor promotion. She was very excited for the opportunity. Henry asked her if she was prepared for the testing or assessment that would likely take place. Her response was interesting. She stated there was no testing or assessment; the selected person was just appointed.

Some agencies might appoint someone to a higher position, but in all his years in law enforcement, Henry only saw law enforcement supervisory promotions use assessments to gauge a candidate's knowledge of departmental policies and procedures. A formal process would ensure everything was fair, and the candidate was capable of meeting the expectations. It is important to assess the abilities of a person who will supervise any organization and lead others, especially when the safety of citizens is at stake. History has shown the desire for society to demand transparency and question the experience of the law enforcement officer during deadly force incidents. The process of promoting preferred but unqualified employees didn't help with employee retention but was often done anyway. The sheriff's office appeared to have the same retention issues as the DA's office.

In 2017, a news story covered new procedures at the county jail which were instituted based on a history of contraband, such as weapons and cellphones, entering the county jail. The county said the new policies would address the problems but left out the fact that jail staff were allegedly supplying the illegal items.

During his time at the DA's office, Henry participated in a detail where sheriff's deputies were under investigation for illegal activity in the jail. The outcome of the investigation was never revealed to investigators working the detail nor to citizens and taxpayers. Although providing an update to investigators or individuals may not be a requirement, the situation raises concern for the safety of other investigators or deputies working with those being investigated. Law enforcement officers, deputies, and other agencies sometimes find themselves working as a team, with each one having access to sensitive information. If a law enforcement person has ethical and moral issues, sensitive information could be relayed about those arrested, serving time, or involved in illegal activity, thus placing other law enforcement persons at risk inside a jail environment or while enforcing law. Even though all sensitive information may not be equally accessible to all law enforcement officers, some information is discussed by word of mouth, making one officer believe another can be trusted with information. There is an understanding that no jail or detention center can expected to be free of contraband, but transparency of the problem was always a concern.

In July 2018, a local newspaper once again printed a story of this anemic and infected county government. More than 18,000 homeowners alleged they were taxed improperly on property taxes—more than $30 million over—and were suing the county.

Appraisers were accused of setting property values with no evaluation of surrounding properties, which resulted in higher values and overtaxation, according to a former tax assessor's board member. The story claims the county refused to provide legal representation for a board member after he was served with a subpoena to appear as a witness. The board member was originally provided outside counsel paid for by the county, but they later withdrew it due to budget constraints. The county also stated the former board member was acting outside of his capacity when the tax information was discovered. The employee's defense was that he was merely looking back at past documents of other assessors where the job was not being done correctly, which could financially hurt taxpayers. The employee also claimed the retraction of legal representation was retaliation for coming forth with the information. The county, just as they had in many other situations, refused to accept responsibility. The county then hired a former Supreme Court chief justice to defend the incident at a cost of more than three hundred dollars per hour. The taxpayers were victims twice, by being overtaxed and then paying attorney fees for the people who robbed them.

CHAPTER 18

How He Made It Through

TREATED AS AN OUTSIDER AS A RESULT of his discrimination complaint, Henry managed to remain steadfast and professional. He spent time many days sending emails to Chief Stoneheart, but he seldom received a response until days later, if one came at all. Coworkers began to isolate themselves from him by ignoring him or treating him as an outcast.

Henry believed other investigators and employees treated him differently because of intimidation by District Attorney Rollins and Stoneheart. Henry had no hard feelings against other employees, as he felt they were only trying to survive and retain their own employment. Henry often thought he would be unable to find opportunities to continue his career after filing a discrimination claim. He felt that the law enforcement profession wanted every member to embrace the good of the profession and remain silent on any immoral or unprofessional acts. Henry accepted there would always be the risk of damage to his reputation. The longer Henry remained employed at the DA's office, the greater the chance those who resented him could compromise his career and reputation. However, it was a chance Henry was willing to take in order to foster change in something bigger than himself.

Henry's strong spiritual background started as a young child. He believed in diversity, fairness, and not limiting his opportunities, and his loving wife of twenty-two years and teenage son provided a very strong source of support. They viewed him as a superhero, the strongest and smartest person they knew. This fueled him daily, even though Henry cried many times, both internally and externally.

Henry had to take a stand and fight for himself and those who didn't have the strength themselves. As a strong believer in prayer, he continuously looked up to his higher power, on his knees, who could move any obstacle that came his way.

It would be impossible to give a single answer as to how Henry made it through. He was very careful with the circle of people he communicated with and the information he allowed himself to be exposed to. He tried constantly to make sure his conversations with others were words of direction, positive and inspiring. Some days nothing seemed to work well because no one had walked in the same shoes who could relate.

Henry found a tremendous amount of relief in professional therapy. Although this was not a magic potion, it provided a neutral ear for him to lay everything out on the table without fear of being judged, assessed, or condemned. Even this was a struggle at times, as it was extremely difficult to speak to a medical professional and explain the behavior and actions of those associated with the criminal justice profession. It's not always easy to manage the emotional and mental rollercoaster of stress, especially when it comes to providing for your family. Henry didn't have many options to avoid the environment at the office.

After applying for well over sixty jobs in his field, Henry was presented with only one opportunity for a phone interview but was never called for a follow-up. He began to believe that his name was floating around in a negative way. He even found himself applying for jobs with vacancies where he was overqualified, but without any luck. This was the moment Henry stepped back and realized that his motivation and determination would not allow him to become totally discouraged.

He had to be even more discreet during work. He never knew when his words would be taken out of context, perceived the wrong way, or intentionally relayed in a negative manner. One day, on the courthouse elevator, he met an old friend and coworker from another police department where both had worked previously. The officer was in a different uniform and employed with a different police agency. Henry asked him how things were going at his new job, and he replied that he absolutely loved it. He felt very comfortable in the position, and the opportunities for advancement were open. Several new officers in the department lacked experience, so he felt his chances of moving up were good.

Approximately two hours later Henry noticed four missed calls from him and a voicemail asking him to call immediately. The man was hysterical, explaining that someone called his command and reported him speaking negatively about the police department at the courthouse. Henry was confused, because he was not sure how he could help, or why he was being told. The person who reported the incident said it occurred on the elevator. After a few minutes of thinking, Henry remembered that another investigator in his office had heard them talking.

This was an investigator with whom Henry had a negative encounter. He had refused to accept evidence from a case that was reassigned to him because the investigator was storing the evidence in her office, which violated evidence chain of custody. If Henry accepted the evidence, knowing the chain of custody rules were violated, he would also be responsible for explaining the history of the evidence in court. The investigator eventually turned the evidence over to a supervisor.

Henry's former coworker asked him to speak to his police supervisor who was given the complaint. Henry had no idea if he was targeted for simply speaking with him or because they had a good relationship. Although Henry had no way to ensure it would help, he reached out to his supervisor and made him aware that the officer did not say anything negative. During the conversation, the supervisor asked him about another investigator at the DA's office and how they were doing. It was the same investigator that he had the evidence conflict with. Henry said he believed the investigator was doing okay and nothing more.

Even on days when Henry felt he had no value at the DA's office, the impact he had on the victims of his cases made him feel otherwise. The DA's office didn't seem to value work, but the victims certainly did. Many of the victims treated him with kindness, as though Henry was their saving grace—but they were his. Victims provided Henry with a focus other than concentrating on the negativity at the DA's office. That was how Henry continued to make it through.

After twenty-three years in the justice system, Henry finally obtained a glimpse of what his ancestors lived through during the civil rights movement by being both overworked and denied. Henry had no intention of voiding his right to speak or make a difference. The truth can be costly, since it holds the possibility of revealing things people are unwilling to accept. Henry developed greater respect for those past and current pioneers. Even though Henry could dictate his ending, standing on principles only a few could accept or understand was a rewarding accomplishment. Some great leaders, such as Dr. Martin Luther King Jr. and Medgar Evers, never saw the end to their beginning, but their achievements will always speak volumes. This was Henry's fuel, his peace, and the drive which allowed him to fight for what he believed in at any level of his life.

Throughout history, we have seen times when accountability and transparency were absent. Police shootings and use of force demand that tools such as police body cameras be used for evidence and transparency. Even with these tools, society remains unsettled with the final legal outcome. When the desire to trust any level of the justice system to be fair, ethical, and transparent fades, a whole new set of issues appear. Even when fatigued over his discrimination claim, Henry found himself able to mentally refuel when he thought about the bigger goal of change and standing up for human rights.

In January 2017, Henry's pastor gave a sermon titled "Inside Power for Outside Pressure," about never allowing the things going on around you to affect who you are. Henry understood how to manage pressure by realizing it was simply a part of life. Some days he felt defeated, while at the same time he determined to do his best as an investigator. Even through all the immoral and unprofessional practices of the DA's office, Henry refused to allow anything to overshadow his work ethic.

At times, people at work as well as citizens Henry encountered while out investigating cases would tell him to smile. Henry was not always sad; he just never had a poker face. Always locked in on his goals and the mission at hand, he acted with professionalism and courtesy, regardless of how he may have appeared. Henry also accepted the actions of others as presenting who they were, unless they did something to prove otherwise. When growing up, many told him he reminded them of his father, who passed away when he was young. His mother told him many stories of his father's diligence to stand for what was right and to protect others.

In the 1960s, one of his older siblings went to the public swimming pool in the small southern town where they lived. When she arrived at the pool, she was not allowed in. His sister returned home and told their father, and in the blink of an eye, he went to the location and addressed those who operated the pool, and later, the city leaders. The pool was eventually closed and never reopened.

Henry never had the opportunity to see his father in action but was confident he did not rest until he made the effort to address the unfair issues. There were other options to closing the pool, such as integration, but in the 1960's South this was not an option, nor was the community open to such a change. It would make sense that swimming privileges should be for everyone or no one at all. Since that time, the town has never had a public pool. Henry was not able to witness all his father's strengths and character firsthand, but there was no doubt his father's DNA resided within him. Throughout his life, Henry has never allowed anyone to devalue him, nor has a day passed where he didn't encourage his children and grandchildren to not just look for change, but to demand it.

CHAPTER 19

Why Henry Took a Stand

SOME EMPLOYEES WITHIN the district attorney's office were forced to live from paycheck to paycheck, while District Attorney Rollins made requests and provisions to approve undisclosed pay raises for specific employees, including himself.

Henry observed these requests within the county's intranet site, which contained investigator forms and resources. Rollins requested approximately $70,000 from a local city's head council member to supplement the salary he was receiving from the county. He justified it by pointing out how many cases he prosecuted for the city as well as the programs he implemented to reduce crime. He also compared his current salary to that of other metropolitan DAs. In April 2020, a local internet news article posted details of Rollins using funds from his nonprofit as a conduit to contribute to his personal salary. The nonprofit was said to be one that Rollins had headed that would reduce youth/gang violence. However, the article highlighted that the nonprofit funds were used to supplement his actual salary as district attorney. According to the article, Rollins received approximately $140,000 in salary from his nonprofit. Rollins's response was that he had secured two financial grants from the local city, paid by his nonprofit. However, Rollins sent a letter to the head councilman requesting a salary increase of approximately $70,000, with no mention of a nonprofit, but only highlighting his efforts to justify a salary increase and no identified or defined specifics of youth or gang violence control. The complaint also stated the ethics commission identified Rollins's violations by his failure to disclose information from his nonprofit. Rollins's statement was that he did not believe the law applied to his busy, atypical nonprofit. The treasurer of Rollins's nonprofit commented that he had nothing to do with the salary process between Rollins and the city and that he would not have done things in that way, which raised questions. In 2020 the state's bureau of investigations division became involved and is now conducting an investigation. This division of the state provides investigative, scientific, and information services and resources to the criminal justice community and others as authorized by law for the purpose of maintaining law. The division conducts criminal investigations along with other criminal justice agencies in the state.

Regardless of the legality of Rollins's actions, Henry couldn't understand how the DA could justify it based on his reasoning. The job of a district attorney is to prosecute cases throughout the county, regardless of how a large city in the county was able to show a decrease in crime. If a raise was warranted for his track record, it should have been provided though the county, just like that of any other employee.

Even the special requests sent to county leaders to raise an individual employee's salaries seemed unfair, especially when no performance evaluations accompanied those requests, and other employees were not included and considered. However, that seemed to be just what DA Rollins wanted. Henry received no performance evaluations during the course of his employment. Assessments could be used to show the differences between employees' performances in order to evaluate for promotions and pay raises. Rollins's salary compensation request from the city occurred while the local police officers for the city had been struggling for years to get any pay increase at all and while county employees were being furloughed.

No one should have to sacrifice their integrity while being required to sit in the midst of unethical practices. Working in the DA's office was the most degrading and embarrassing experience Henry had experienced in his career. To be sexually discriminated against was the equivalent of being racially discriminated against, because Henry had no control over his gender, just as one would have no control over the color of their skin.

The county government, later excluded from the discrimination claim and lawsuit by the courts, was just as much to blame, in Henry's opinion. Although the DA was an elected official, the county should be familiar, through documentation, of how employees were promoted, hired, or ended their employment in order to address any concerns or patterns.

Through conversations with others, Henry found that the DA's office did conduct exit interviews, but he wondered if they placed any value on them or whether they were even offered to all. Henry spoke with many investigators who resigned, and several shared the same concerns he did. Some of them said they refused to participate in an exit interview because they didn't feel it would change anything. This would make sense for those individuals who did not want to risk damaging their careers.

Each day, Henry thought how citizens deserved the right to know how their elected district attorney was allowing his office to function and how his conduct was accepted by the county. Henry kept himself aware not only of concerns with the DA's office, but also with the entire county, since it affected how the office operated.

One incident involved a mayor in the county and a vendor for the city's airport. Funds were allocated by the city for the vendor to purchase a vehicle for use in airport business. A discrepancy was discovered between the amount of money spent for the vehicle purchase and the amount documented by the vendor. This could have been deception or an error in calculation. If it was deception, it was subject to criminal charges in the county. Depending on the dollar value, criminal charges could range from a misdemeanor charge of less than one year in jail to a felony charge of more than a year.

The vendor, a close friend of the mayor, submitted an invoice for approximately $25,000 after purchasing the vehicle. However, it was alleged that the actual price of the vehicle was less than the invoice, and the vendor kept the balance for himself. The case was presented to the DA's office to be considered for prosecution. DA Rollins reviewed it and decided that no crime was committed because the money was returned; however, according to the reports, this occurred after the investigation began.

Once it was determined that the decision was made by Rollins not to prosecute, a government watchdog that targeted immoral and unethical government practices stated that the incident was one elected official looking out for another. Although there were never any charges by the local police, it was normal to present incidents to the district attorney for consideration to prosecute. Rollins didn't have much to say and resented the questioning by the media, adding that some questions were out of bounds.

Rollins stated that the incident could be viewed as a theft where the two parties came to an agreement. The vendor may have reached an agreement with the city. If the citizens were victims, the decision was bigger than could be resolved outside of the courtroom.

In 2017, Chief Stoneheart announced that a new female investigator with less than one year of tenure would replace the supervisor, who decided to resign his employment and work for another DA's office. There was also an announcement that Litia Sampson would become supervisor of another unit, which handled sex trafficking duties. This was confusing to Henry as well as other investigators, because Sampson had received the position at the center of Henry's discrimination complaint. Now she was promoted to supervisor of a unit that consisted only of her, with no one to supervise, as she was the only person performing the sex trafficking duties related to the position.

Several weeks later, Stoneheart asked to meet with all supervisors, including those who were new. After the meeting, an email was sent by the new supervisor of Henry's division informing everyone of a 1:00 p.m. meeting. During the meeting she said that while she had only one year in the division, she had twenty years in law enforcement. It appeared she was justifying why she was promoted, even though Henry and one other investigator in the division had more than twenty years of experience and more tenure, and neither were considered. While there may be other experiences that can prepare an individual to manage and supervise others, Chief Stoneheart continued to make advancement decisions without seeking others who were qualified.

Some of those Henry worked with who became aware of his efforts to promote change and fairness might have thought he had turned against the criminal justice profession, even after serving for over twenty years. He never wanted anything given to him, nor was he given anything in his career, but he worked hard and gave his all to the profession. So, Henry chose to try and bring an end to the discrimination and unfair practices at the office. He wanted a fair opportunity to advance his career while helping victims heal.

If changes are not making people better, then they are not truly changing. Ineffective leaders groomed by the DA's office never managed to produce effective and valuable changes. Issues were shuffled around by supervisors and management like a deck of cards. When there is no defined set of ethical measures, actions, and standards, it leaves room for manipulation. The office's set of moral and ethical standards were vague. Henry understood that he would never convince the DA's office that he was correct in standing for fairness, but he did believe that his commitment to hold them accountable would drive change for the future. His ultimate goal was to expose their past behavior to prevent future incidents.

Some days Henry wondered how he could know when people were really in his corner. He decided it was when people support and respect what he believed in, even when they didn't always agree. Henry encourages all who face discrimination, harassment, or unfair treatment to release themselves, tell their stories, and hold those responsible to account.

CHAPTER 20

Does the System Work?
Or Is It the Problem?

THROUGH THE COURSE OF HIS DISCRIMINATION CASE, Henry read about the stories of several individuals who attempted to file cases of workplace rights violations. An overwhelmingly large number of cases were said to have never been investigated by the Equal Employment Opportunity Commission (EEOC), which is the first stage in the process of filing federal cases of discrimination and harassment. Henry believed that anyone who filed claims through their job rather than through the EEOC would not be evaluated fairly, if at all.

It is common as a first option for most places of employment to provide policies and procedures for employees to file suspected violations internally through Human Resources or through staff designated to investigate such violations. In this situation, Henry believed that filing via the employer posed the risk of the employer denying it because they were looking out for their own best interests.

Paychex Worx, a company that provides a variety of business resources including finance marketing, human resources, benefits, and capital management, provided some interesting statistics online.

The 2019 article showed a total of forty-eight states that have laws related to equal pay, excluding Alabama and Mississippi at that time, with Georgia requiring at least ten employees to enforce equal pay laws. A twenty-one-year analysis from 1997 to 2018 showed 1.8 million complaints filed. Out of these, 63% showed no issues; 18% administratively closed, 8.1% through settlement; 4.8% of complainants withdrew; 3.2% were considered for legal action; and 1.4% reached an informal solution. The most recent year data was provided was 2018, which showed 1,889,631 discrimination complaints were filed, with 2017 numbers providing a breakdown of complaints into categories. The largest number of complaints were for retaliation, at 49%; race, 34%; disability, 34%; and sex, above 30%. Another article showed concern that cases were not being investigated at all by the EEOC, according to the Center for Public Integrity. The article stated cases were being closed without investigation due to lack of staff and resources. The 2019 article mentioned that since 2008, the complaints had doubled from agencies that were defined to be on the low-list priority, such as the government, where no mediation or probe for facts had taken place. Even though backlogged cases were said to be improved by 30%, only 13% of 2018 cases, prior to the article, led to a case being settled or providing some type of relief for the complainant, which was lower than in 2008, ten years earlier. The EEOC's statement expressed that more time was being taken early on to collect information for cases which were stronger in order to get assistance. The agency had a reported 26,000 cases placed in the high-priority pool, which was said to have increased since 1996. It appeared to be a fine line between high- and low-priority cases. However, Henry believed that priority made no difference to a victim, and they all deserved attention.

When Henry filed against the district attorney's office, he was passionate in gaining an understanding of how the process had gone for others and how it would likely go for him. It was understandable how the process could appear confusing. The initial process for him consisted of writing up a claim and turning it into the local EEOC, where Henry was given a claim identification number and told it would be assigned to an investigator. The investigator would determine whether the claim met the elements for which it was filed.

As an employee of the justice system, Henry knew the importance of having assistance from a professional, such as an attorney, to help navigate the stressful process. However, he only wondered what would happen with those who attempted to address discrimination issues with no understanding of laws and without the ability to obtain guidance or representation from an attorney. As a criminal investigator, Henry understood that the burden of proof that a crime was committed rests upon the prosecutor. If evidence showed that no other reasonable person could have committed the crime other than the defendant, then the burden was met.

Civil claims require only what is legally known as the "preponderance of evidence," or a 50 percent chance that the evidence is true compared to proof beyond a doubt, as with evidence of a crime. Prior to the filing, Henry secured an attorney who specialized in civil rights cases. His attorney explained that there is a specific timeline in which the investigator has to provide responses to claims. If there is no response, the claimant is then granted the right to file a lawsuit. At the end of August 2016, Henry was told by his attorney that the DA's office was granted an extension to reply to his claim. This was the same pattern as the other cases Henry had read about that had long delays and a lack of updates. The EEOC allows claimants to check the status of the claim online, but the information is limited, usually only telling whether the case is being processed. Henry received no change in his status for months. This gave the appearance of transparency without providing any useful information.

Henry thought about this case as if he were investigating a criminal case. If the investigator didn't pursue or document the facts of his case with his claim, the chances were greater that it would be ruled invalid or damages would be kept to a minimum. Henry also wondered if the EEOC was actually neutral. In November 2016, Henry learned from his attorney that both his initial discrimination complaint and the retaliation compliant filed later were due for a response in December. If the DA's office failed to meet the deadline, they would be issued a subpoena. Henry also received a certified letter in November from the county department that investigates employee claims. They offered him the opportunity to speak with them and said they would be reaching out to him. It was the same letter sent to him when he filed his initial complaint. On the advice of his attorney, Henry declined to participate, and told them he would let the EEOC complete its investigation.

In January 2017 the county finally provided a response to both claims and denied any acts of discrimination. Henry was able to review the responses, which were completely deceptive and untruthful. They claimed there was no discrimination in giving the position, which was a promotion, to a woman without a formal process, and that Henry had not expressed interest. It was also alleged that the position had been open to candidates on a temporary basis until it could be filled permanently. Chief Stoneheart didn't make any announcements or request any resumes until being served with the claim. This appeared the best the county could come up with after months of delays.

Soon after, Henry was informed by his attorney that the assigned investigator explained he was unable to complete an investigation within the 180-day timeframe designated to complete all complaints, and therefore the investigator was issuing a "right to sue" notice be provided. However, the final approval had to come from the justice department in Washington D.C. Henry was never able to grasp how the justice department could review an attempt to receive justice when no real facts to the incident were investigated. Henry spoke with a former colleague who filed a claim with the EEOC after being terminated from his job as a police officer. The former officer said that after months of hearing nothing, he was finally granted the right to sue, but the notice didn't mean his department had done anything wrong. This was the same response given when his right to sue notice was provided, by noting that the letter did not confirm liable actions by his agency. The officer hired an attorney after receiving the notification, but his termination was upheld. He did not discuss the determining factors of why the termination was upheld, but he believed the lack of assistance in navigating the process caused him to lose the claim.

Our nation is one that prides itself on fairness, on justice, and on being the greatest nation. It leaves one to wonder if our system of democracy is being compromised by those we trust—criminal justice agencies—who are sworn to enforce law and provide justice, but who do so with bias and prejudice.

The initial filing is a major step in the process of receiving justice, as it helps establish the foundation of the complaint. It seems many victims lack a clear understanding of the role the employment commission plays when seeking justice. Henry believed the position of the commission was to be neutral and serve as potential fact finders with investigation. This leaves those who file claims to be placed in the position of filing the claim alone if they don't have attorneys, and to do their own investigation to help gather and submit the necessary facts to be considered. Once a claim is filed, the information used to file the claim is the major tool used to consider the validity of the complaint. If there is a lack of guidance in preparing a good complaint, which could require basic writing skills or articulation of facts, the foundation of the claim could be useless before it's ever considered by the employment commission. Whether or not an employee is treated fairly should not depend on their ability to explain, but rather on the facts, which someone should advocate to explain. Providing a criminal attorney to advocate on your behalf is a constitutional right; however, having someone aid and advocate for your employment rights may seem to come at the cost of either securing an attorney or being forced to seek justice alone.

Henry wondered where the *true* justice was. If there were concerns about preventing bad behavior in the future, how could it be done while ensuring that no stone is left unturned? Henry always felt civil cases pursued against government agencies were not treated the same as cases against private businesses or individuals. When a government agency is pursued for civil violations, it risks losing the public's trust and confidence if clues are confirmed. There should be no less effort to obtain truth whether it concerns employees or citizens. It disturbed Henry that states implement laws that cap the amount of money awarded to victims who sue the government, whereas there are no caps for civil damages related to companies or individuals. Even if a case was given a right-to-sue notice, Henry felt there was no desire to deter the behavior, but only to provide some hope for justice. Have we perhaps reached a point where the negative behavior of those in the justice system have not only created concerns for those employed or those they service, but also for the social justice concerns that society routinely faces? Perhaps we have reached a crossroad where concerns can no longer be treated as meritless, frivolous, or without cause; instead, investigations are a must, to hold all involved to present facts so truth can be discovered.

Those who discriminate and violate the civil rights of others are aware of the laws; however, they choose to assess how violations will benefit their needs at that moment. He strongly feels that efforts to end discrimination begin with challenging each and every violator and those who aid them.

CHAPTER 21

The Final Battle Begins

As Henry set out to raise awareness through this book, he wanted readers to understand that he was not an investigator who was terminated and then decided to raise his voice. He could have remained quiet and stayed on the job while receiving a decent salary. He could have, like many others, avoided speaking out. The fact is, he could no longer believe in the criminal justice system as it was and what it claimed to represent.

Henry was not sure where this decision would lead him, but he vowed to continue as long as it blazed a path for truth and allowed others to see the light. He was aware that many wanted to put an end to the problems in the district attorney's office but did not understand how to act. He was also aware of those who question their own abilities based on a culture of being treated without value. After witnessing acts of bullying, immoral practices, and workplace discrimination, it became obvious how it damaged the confidence of employees.

In November 2016 Henry sent an email request to the chief investigator and his supervisor requesting a change in his hours. He needed to arrive an hour earlier and leave an hour earlier in order to complete the last class he needed to receive his degree in criminal justice. This was very important to him. Not only was it a personal achievement, it opened the door to other career opportunities. With Stoneheart's history of not responding to his emails, Henry attached return receipts. His supervisor read the message the same day, and Stoneheart read the message the next day. Neither of them responded immediately. Two days later, his supervisor told him Stoneheart had approved his request. This was a concern, because the office had a tendency to give verbal responses instead of written ones, leaving them the ability to recant the statement at a later date.

In early 2017 Henry took the time to sit back to evaluate the journey he was going through. Although he applied for several jobs in his field after filing the discrimination case, he often wondered if he could work in law enforcement or government any longer, even though he had to earn a living. This grieved him, because he had invested more than twenty years of his life in the profession and could not imagine doing anything different—this was his passion. As Henry got closer to completing his degree with the goal of managing and leading others, he thought deeply about how it might turn out. It had become very difficult to support the justice system after witnessing it fail in so many ways. One individual cannot change a broken system, and yet nothing changes unless someone speaks up. Henry felt the justice system needed direction and a reestablishment of trust, just as one would guide a child in building and mainlining good character—to do the right thing, even when no one is watching.

Near the end of February 2017, the entire county government, including the DA's office, tried to appear moral and ethical by establishing a confidential, anonymous system of reporting fraud and ethics violations committed by employees. There was also a third-party hotline to collect reports. Examples of reportable violations included improper use of funds, falsification of documents, kickbacks, theft of cash or county property, conflicts of interest, and misuse of county time and resources. These were the only issues offered, so Henry wasn't sure if any other violations were open to be reported. Henry didn't believe the county was honest and sincere with this endeavor. Based on past experience, they were having a difficult time managing the concerns they created. No information

Southern Justice

was available on who would review the reports and data from those who reported them, but only that the information was collected by a third party. Henry felt the reports would go directly to someone in the county to implement damage control rather than to punish offenders. Any retaliation against an employee who called the hotline was strictly prohibited, according to the notification. If this was a confidential resource, where were the guidelines regarding who would review the contents and take action against the violators or those who retaliated?

In early March 2017 Henry's attorney informed him that his claim had cleared all necessary obstacles, and they could move to the phase of filing a lawsuit. The next month, Henry interviewed for a job as director of security at a private company, one of many jobs he had applied for. This would be a much-needed opportunity, as Henry had decided this portion of the criminal justice system was no longer a passion for him. Like many of the opportunities Henry pursued while going through his legal case, this one did not yield success. Even though Henry was now at the stage of filing a lawsuit, no amount of money would restore his confidence in the DA's office. Henry also believed they were eager to relieve themselves of the situation and of him. Stoneheart was practicing subtle acts such as ignoring Henry's emails, being unprofessional, and creating conflicts when Henry complied with policies and laws related to issues such as managing evidence. Even when procedures and policies supported the way Henry performed in his job, Stoneheart attempted to use her authority and power to discourage his job performance.

Each day consisted of assignments and small tasks designed to make him uncomfortable, fatigued, or just plain frustrated. However, his quest was always to take the high road and maintain professionalism. In May, Henry had finally seen it all.

While Henry prepared a case for trial, Stoneheart stopped by his office and asked if he could sit in on an interview for potential investigators. Henry almost dropped to the floor in shock and disbelief. It took him a minute to process how she could ask him to participate in an interview panel when the process involved

171

highlighting and discussing the positives of a job in order to recruit potential applicants. Henry also believed Stoneheart made attempts to see how professional he could remain, regardless of the request or task she presented. In an effort to be professional, Henry gracefully accepted. As he stood, she revealed her reason for requesting him, stating that there was no one else in the office who was available. It was uncomfortable sitting before a panel of potential applicants and seeing them pursue what Henry believed to be a dead-end job.

During the interview, Stoneheart told one of the candidates that the position would accompany a salary greater than what Henry was making. The candidate's resume contained a block of training that gave him the opportunity to receive a salary comparable to a senior investigator. This training was no more advanced than Henry's, when comparing both their areas of expertise.

In July 2017, Henry's attorney completed all documents and filed his lawsuit. There were no positive changes made at the DA's office and no change in his decision to seek other employment. In early July, Henry was hit with one final jolt to his efforts to make an exit from this dreadful place into a new career. Even though his goal was to obtain peace while waiting for the legal process to resolve, Henry still anticipated a clean slate for a new career. He had yet another door close when he received a call that another applicant had been selected for a job he had pursued. It was more than just the loss of another opportunity. At this point, Henry believed that he was on someone's blacklist. In his twenty-plus years as a law enforcement professional, he felt as though protecting the "thin blue line" really existed, and nobody was allowed to challenge the system. As fast as Henry felt devastated by this rejection, a light came on inside him, revealing that this door closing, and all those before it, were signs they were not meant to be.

Later that month, his lawsuit was officially filed in federal court. Henry anticipated this would produce new forms of harassment and retaliation, since it was a step closer to accountability. After a long fight of overcoming challenges in the DA's office, he and his wife decided it was time to shift environments in pursuit of peace of mind. Henry presented his office with a letter of resignation at the beginning of August. Although Henry felt instant relief, a part of him believed he had lost the battle by other means. This battle was not so much one that involved those who negatively impacted his career but was rather the fight for victims of crime. Henry never thought he would see the day that serving and protecting people would come to an end for him. Even with his feelings about losing this battle, Henry was optimistic about winning the war.

A couple of weeks later Henry conducted his office inventory, exited for the last time, and felt free for the first time in years. Relief came in knowing that the one environment that had changed his life in so many ways was forced to release its grip. Even though unsure of his next step, Henry felt sure he would not regret his decision to leave the past negative experiences in the district attorney's office behind him. He was convinced this was the worst experience of his entire life, but it had made him stronger. Henry could now peacefully await the next phase of receiving justice and pray that others would follow with the same courage. Henry entered as a professional and exited as a professional up to the last hour, after most employees had left the building to begin their weekend.

Near the end of August, Henry and his family ventured off to a new beginning. They put their home on the market and moved over eight hundred miles away. Within a few days of placing their home up for sale, they received an offer and closed at the end of September. Henry was still without employment to assist with his transition, but they had faith that the efforts to take a stand and seek justice would prevail. The long drive was fatiguing, but their peace of mind improved as Henry moved closer to his new beginning. Once they arrived and settled in, an even greater peace came over Henry. He could actually begin in a new environment with a new start and not be judged on his actions to stand up for what he believed. As he mingled among people from day-to-day, he felt liberated and equal.

Shortly after his arrival, Henry received a phone call from a former investigator in the county he had left. This person was in the process of filing a lawsuit against the DA's office for improper termination. He also mentioned that he and several other employees were displeased with the way Henry had been treated, including the incident involving the promotion given to the investigator less qualified. He suggested Henry call his own attorney in reference to filing a lawsuit as well, stating that he believed others who had been treated unfairly could join the attempt to prevent the unfair treatment.

Henry was not sure whether this person knew he had a pending case or simply wanted to discuss how he was treated, along with the details of why he left. Many at the office had begun treating Henry differently after he filed the lawsuit—not talking to him and keeping their distance—but another investigator mentioned to Henry before he left that she knew about the lawsuit and she believed he did the right thing. Henry did not engage in much conversation with the investigator he was speaking with, but merely listened. He did not want to discuss either his case or the investigator's case without knowing the facts.

As Henry continued to get settled, he considered his new career plans and where he would go from there. He took some time to sit back and get his bearings. After a few months he began looking for employment. The search was slow, as Henry was still struggling with the decision on whether to pursue law enforcement or criminal justice opportunities. Even though Henry was in a new place, his previous experiences left him unsettled and unsure. He felt free from the environment he had left, but even the thought of pursuing a career in the justice system made him ponder whether the entire system was broken.

While determining which route he wanted to go, he accepted security jobs in the private sector rather than government positions. Between 2017 and 2018, Henry worked at a school system and a hospital, attempting to find a good fit, but he discovered this wasn't what he was looking for as a career. In the summer of 2018 Henry was blessed with an opportunity to become the director of security for a wonderful company. He was finally able to have an employer who understood his value and accepted him as a professional. This provided him and his family the feeling that they were headed in the right direction. Although he had a long road still ahead in his lawsuit, he felt this new job would help him endure the ongoing legal fight.

In February 2018 his attorney said the process was set to move into the discovery of evidence phase, after a judge denied the county's attempts to have the claim dismissed. The time where his truth would be heard and those accountable would face justice was near. Henry stayed abreast of what was happening at the DA's office through local news reports and those still employed there.

During the first week of May 2018 Henry was able to review a set of discovery evidence information, which were interrogatory responses. These are questions prepared by an attorney to show what is expected to be asked during a deposition. The person deposed is expected to give the same responses under oath in front of a court reporter if the process reaches that point. Interrogatory responses present no surprises as long as the person is honest, and the person answering is allowed to have representation to guide them. Even though depositions are not formal, each participant must be truthful, as the document is a writing that is under the terms of an oath. The responses are filed and can be used in court, just as evidence would be.

Henry read Stoneheart's responses first and determined after the first one that the DA's office was fighting a battle that they were sure to lose. She was asked to confirm or deny that she had spoken to him in a one-on-one meeting where she said she needed a female for the human trafficking position and females were better for it. She denied making the statement, and this would be a major piece of evidence in the case. His attorney was in possession of audio evidence confirming she did make that statement. The damaging response not only showed that Stoneheart discriminated, but that she also lied on a writing of oath by not responding truthfully. DA Rollins was asked to confirm whether any family members worked in the surrounding area and to identify all personal and work email addresses and cell phone numbers used during a certain time frame. His response was vague, stating that obtaining information was burdensome and too broad, and that email and cellphone information was controlled by the county. Henry believed his attorney team wanted to be thorough and aware of any identified relationships which could show bias or favor toward discriminatory practices specific to the position of which he was denied. The information would also display any communication which supported the discriminatory act.

In June, it was Henry's turn to respond to questions from the defense team representing Rollins and Stoneheart. Henry was asked to explain how the DA's office discriminated and retaliated against him. He responded that Stoneheart said a female was needed for the job, and that they are better for the position. Henry explained that after being served with a discrimination complaint, the DA's office posted a position with strategically changed qualifications from any other investigator position in the office, past or present, that he had ever received copies of, and which exceeded his qualifications. It was later confirmed by the county's personnel department that no such position existed, and that it was posted after the discrimination claim was filed. The job appeared to be an effort to show that applicants were sought. Henry thought this response was damaging for the chief investigator, district attorney, and the defense team of the county. According to the personnel department representative Henry spoke with, every open position must be approved through the county before it can be a recognized position with the county, and the posted position was not approved. The initial position that Henry was denied was never posted or opened to qualified applicants, and it was an approved position through the county. The position was filled with a woman each time it came open.

In May 2018, Henry had the opportunity to attend a training seminar. It covered diversity and inclusion in the workplace and society. One statement made by the instructor carried more power than any training, lecture, or even speech: "Diversity is being asked or offered to come to the dance; inclusion is being asked to dance. If even one of us are denied the opportunity to dance, in any capacity or scope, they are discriminated against, regardless of the efforts used to deceive the human eye."

His deposition was scheduled for October, and the only question that remained was how long the county would continue the fight once Henry spoke the words of truth. The depositions were delayed for a few weeks, but once they resumed, Rollins would be first and Stoneheart a few days later. Henry observed their depositions over Skype. The demeanor and actions of Rollins were just as Henry expected. He began the deposition aggressively, refusing to give his home address as part of the introduction. After a brief conference, Rollins complied with the process and shrunk from his kingdom of power and control. He testified that he was the sole person who made hiring and promotion decisions, but he accepted recommendations from Stoneheart and other managers. When asked about his hiring process, he was vague and evasive. He would only state that vacant positions within his office were communicated to the county's Human Resources department to be filled.

Henry's attorney asked him if it was normal to have no idea of his hiring process if he made the sole decision on who was hired or promoted. Rollins attempted to regroup, saying he guessed he would look at the qualifications of the applicant to see if they were a good fit. Henry's attorney asked him for the documented process of hiring or promoting employees. He wasn't able to offer any and admitted there was no documented process.

When asked about Henry's qualifications for the position he was denied, Rollins stated Henry was very qualified but did not seem motivated and interested. He was also questioned about his failure to acknowledge Henry's request to speak with him about his interest in the position. The request was made to Rollins's executive assistant, who was responsible for setting his appointment calendar. After inquiring why Henry's appointment wasn't granted, Rollins confirmed that he allowed the assistant to decide which appointments were granted. Henry had made the request to speak with him via email to his assistant, which was standard practice, but never received a response from either the assistant or Rollins. Henry questioned how an assistant could decide who could speak with the DA.

Rollins made every effort to separate Stoneheart from any of the hiring and promoting responsibilities. He also made efforts to detach himself at the same time, by stating that there were times that the county occasionally denied his requests to hire or promote employees. When asked about these incidents by Henry's attorney, Rollins could not produce any evidence of denials, nor could he articulate a process for hiring or promotions. If no process existed, then Henry concluded his actions were personal wishes of either DA Rollins and/or Chief Stoneheart and were not based on providing a fair process.

Rollins was untruthful when he said Henry only wanted the promotion as a stepping-stone to transition to the homicide division in the DA's office. Henry never had any interest and had not taken any initiative to move to a division related to working homicides. He was asked a year prior by Stoneheart if he would consider leaving his division working sexual assault cases after the supervisor of the division requested him. Henry informed her that he was not interested but was only interested in the position for which he was denied the opportunity. Rollins was attempting to demonstrate that Henry was not interested in the position denied to him; therefore, no discrimination would have occurred.

Once Rollins's deposition was complete, it was time for Stoneheart, and Henry watched again via Skype, two days later. Henry's attorney addressed her with questions, and she was vague about dates and times when she would have announced open positions under her authority. She followed up by saying that the office does not document any formal process, because promotions are only in-house.

Henry's attorney then asked her if Henry was qualified for the position. Her response was that it depended on the definition of "qualified." She added that some positions are not about how qualified you are. Stoneheart attempted to explain that she felt victims of sexual crimes may not feel comfortable speaking to males and using words like "vagina," even though Henry was hired by the DA's office for his expertise with sexual assault cases and to work in the sexual assault division there. She also said Henry just did not seem interested in the position, failing to acknowledge the email he sent her doing just that. If Henry had been serious about the position, she explained, he would have approached her personally after receiving no reply.

The most critical part of the deposition came when Henry's attorneys presented a disc to Stoneheart's defense team. It contained evidence showing her admitting she only selected a woman for the job because, in her words, "she needed a female." The audio also confirmed her saying that "females are better for the job," "some days are just not your day," and "some jobs are just not your job." Even her demeanor on the audio was unprofessional, revealing her use of profanity. The defense attorney, of course, immediately objected to the audio being played, but the audio was allowed. As it played, Henry could see Stoneheart become nervous. Before it was finished, she lost control of her emotions.

"So this was a set up!" she yelled. "I guess you was just trying to sue! Well, you got what you wanted!"

Henry's attorney paused the audio and asked Stoneheart if the voice on the audio was, in fact, hers, which she confirmed. The recording continued as she attempted to justify giving the position to a woman by alleging that she had more seniority, which was not true. Stoneheart even insisted that maybe there were other jobs that might interest Henry. Although Henry felt he had been kicked in the stomach when she made the comment in person, Henry gathered himself and remained poised. He made acknowledgments that he understood, along with other small talk captured on the audio recording. Even though he had heard the recording many times, each time rekindled the anger and disappointment. The depositions reopened every wound and mental bruise that had resulted from the discrimination.

After the deposition was completed, Henry's attorney informed him that Stoneheart told him during a brief break that when he sees Henry, to tell him, "What goes around, comes around!" Henry's attorney treated this information as a potential threat and had the court reporter put the statement on record.

In December 2018 Henry's attorney contacted him with even more damaging information against the county. Litia Sampson, the investigator given the promotion that led to all this, agreed to sign a declaration confirming there was never any intent to give Henry the promotion. The declaration summarized that after his claim was filed, Sampson was contacted by Stoneheart and informed that she had to interview for the position. Stoneheart told Sampson that there was no risk of losing the position, but the complaint made the interview necessary. Sampson concluded by saying there was never any mention that her position was temporary.

Henry knew the day would finally come when individuals like Rollins and Stoneheart would no longer be allowed to control others with power and fear, nor would they be allowed to stand on the top of their mountain and spit down on others. Their careers would not go unblemished.

CHAPTER 22

The Verdict

IN LATE FEBRUARY 2019 it would be Henry's turn to tell the facts at his deposition. The county attorney for DA Rollins and Chief Stoneheart made every effort to show that Rollins was the ultimate decision-maker when it came to the hiring and promoting process, not Stoneheart. However, she was insistent in the recorded meeting where she made the discriminatory statements that she was the one in charge and made the decisions.

The defense attorney for Rollins and Stoneheart asked Henry who he thought made the decision to deny him a promotion. Henry answered that he felt it was Stoneheart, believing that anyone who made such bold statements had the ability to make decisions. The strategy of the attorney to relieve Stoneheart of any culpability seemed to be failing.

The defense attorney asked Henry many different questions suggesting Rollins made the decisions, such as who signed certain documents and who hired him. But assistants often used a stamp with the DA's name on it to approve documents such as expenditure reports. This did not mean they oversaw or were in charge of approving the document, only that they had authorization from the DA to complete the process with his approval by stamping. Rollins could not deny his part in actions done by his assistants, as it was his responsibility to set expectations between himself and his assistants. Regardless of how documents were signed and approved, Rollins had designated his responsibilities and duties without a structured process of oversight. Without this structured process, Rollins would be able to deny incidents or events which could later show him as responsible for (or a contributor to) an outcome that was negative or adverse. After every question asked of Henry in regard to who held decision-making power, he paused, squared his shoulders, and looked the attorney firmly in the eyes, answering that Stoneheart made the decision to not promote him. Rollins was still involved, as he was aware and supported her, rubber-stamping all of Stoneheart's decisions. This was why she had the arrogance to do and say as she pleased.

Just before the completion of the deposition, Henry was provided with additional information that could potentially be used as evidence. His attorney discovered emails that were sent during the time of his discrimination. An administrative employee of the county sent an email to Stoneheart asking her to tailor the job description for whatever she needed. That description was the one posted by DA Rollins's office manager containing strict qualifications that differed from any other investigator position in the office. Most important was the metadata, which contained a history of what happened to the email, showing it was deleted after the courts made the request that all emails relative to the case be turned over. This information was preserved by his attorney in the event it would be needed for a trial. It showed that the county was not only unethical with their discrimination, but also corrupt in trying to destroy evidence.

About a week after his deposition, Henry received news from his attorney that the defense and the county had decided to halt any further proceedings and was considering a resolution. Henry believes his experience, professionalism, and endurance will forever guide those who struggle to come forward, stand up to others, and do what's right. The movement to stop unethical behavior by government agencies, employees, and leaders has never been more real. Although there are deadlines to file complaints, speaking up and doing the right thing has no expiration date.

Relief flowed through Henry as he moved toward closing this chapter in his life. A mental and physical burden had been lifted. He could now hold those responsible to account for negatively impacting his career and that of others. To those who fall prey to such behavior, Henry would say to be strong and committed, but most of all, to remain diligent. If anyone makes the decision to take a stand, Henry encourages them to be confident, direct, and to stand with dignity. We must never forget that the constitution and the justice system do not define us. We define them, by ensuring that both represent all who encounter them. It will be uncomfortable to bring civil claims against those who violate the constitution they swore to uphold, but it is a must, to promote confidence in the justice system.

Henry never looks to gain popularity; he only hopes to bring forth courage in those who are lacking. He wonders where the criminal justice system is headed in our nation. We have been forced to live in a world where police officers must use tools such as body cameras to produce transparency and maintain integrity. But what safeguards us against a DA's office whose integrity is in question by knowingly discriminating and attempting to cover it up? If there is no trust in those who prosecute criminal offenders, who can we trust to uphold justice? Remember, any individual who loses credibility will immediately and forever compromise the system they represent.

In mid-April 2019, Henry's case went through court-ordered mediation, and both sides were able to come to an agreement. After the mediation was over, Henry left that chapter and career behind him. Nothing about the solution gave Henry any hope that the DA's office or Rollins and Stoneheart's leadership would change. But Henry believes we must raise our voices and expose acts of discrimination.

If the highest leaders in the criminal justice system can't be trusted, we will never be able to end discriminatory work practices.

We simply cannot have tunnel vision focused on those who commit criminal acts, while treating the violation of civil rights as less important. When a person's civil rights are violated, their lives can be impacted and changed forever, just as those of a victim of violent crime. Nobody talks about how victims of civil rights violations will suffer and what their outcome will be. We will never be a nation free of discrimination until we identify all discrimination, hold all accountable, and punish those who offend. Exposure does promote some individual accountability and opens other considerations for change.

During Henry's time at the DA's office, he witnessed a seesaw of ethical and unethical practices. The county's biggest defense during his lawsuit was that Rollins was the highest decision-maker, not Stoneheart. She sparked the discrimination claim, but Rollins believed the defense was to remove any decision-making abilities from Stoneheart because of the discriminatory audio statement. However, the statement also displayed the confidence and arrogance with her personal decisions to choose who she wanted to promote. Rollins drove the discriminatory practices while attempting to manage employees through fear and control. He relinquished his power only when the situation would not benefit him. Henry believed most people who accepted Rollins's demands had no idea that their actions could lead them to act illegally or could negatively impact careers. Employees under his control either wanted to carry out his wishes or were intimidated, ultimately going down a path of prejudiced behavior.

All these actions had the ability to destroy lives and careers, affecting even criminal cases. After Henry's case was resolved and summary details made public through an online news media source, Henry read a social media post from a former assistant district attorney that worked under DA Rollins. The post mentioned the attorney remembering the days of working in the office, when Rollins picked who would assist on cases based on race instead of merit or experience. In providing and upholding justice, nothing allows Rollins a defense of his discriminatory actions and beliefs or his internalized practice of racism and oppression. If a DA's office can operate this way, how are we to trust they will extend fair and equal justice toward victims and defendants? Americans have always embraced the power of voting to drive change within the justice system. However, the true engine for change is to blow apart and expose the cultures and beliefs that feed the fiery beasts of disparity, discrimination, and inequalities within the justice system. When we simply change the faces of those who balance the scales of justice, we are only shifting the ghost of the past from one regime to the next. The process of appointing leaders as favors *must* become a thing of the past before justice reform can even begin. It is time to focus not on what individuals in the justice system can do for one another, but on how they can best impact justice and fairness for the greater good of society.

Addressing discrimination is far from a new idea, but it is a realistic one that can only be made successful by those who truly desire to end discriminatory practices. America, these issues are real, they are active, and they are TODAY!

Afterword

One mild, sunny day in June 2016, Henry Blaze Wisper stood up to unfair, discriminatory practices as an employee of the criminal justice system and embarked on a path for change. He took on a district attorney's office and government entity in the Southeastern region of the United States, seeking to expose and end an environment of favoritism and unfair employee and prosecutorial practices.

Discrimination, prejudice, and corruption in our criminal justice system have severely damaged the constitution's foundation. The DA's office and the county avoided transparency, opting for a standard practice of deception. Our justice system is composed of several entities at its core: police, courts, and prisons. When any level of the core is weakened, it damages the entire system we believe in and is perhaps not repairable.

Henry, a dedicated professional, gave twenty-three years of his life before the system he believed in negatively impacted his career. The system damaged crime victims, county employees, and defendants. Employees of these institutions take oaths to serve and protect while earnestly seeking the truth. The primary job of the DA's office and its employees is to protect the core values of our justice system and constitution. However, many were playing the role of defendant, pointing the finger at others.

Society continues to struggle with doing what is popular and comfortable as opposed to what is just and righteous. When justice prevails over darkness and evil, it creates a bright light with a path for others to follow. Without equality in every part of an agency's justice system, the system is without justice. These are the concerns tearing apart the fragile garment of our nation. However, the issues of our justice system have always been much bigger than one entity and one incident. These practices will continue until we unite toward healing, not just through these written words but with uplifted voices to force transparency.

ABOUT THE AUTHOR

Governor Henderson Jr. is a Midwesterner with a devoted wife of over twenty years and a teenage son, both of whom he has committed his life to. As a military veteran, his values consist of pride, commitment, and respect. Having spent two decades working in the criminal justice system, he understands the struggles that society must balance in regard to fair justice for both victims and the accused. But his concern is to ensure that those who uphold justice are moral, ethical, and honest, as no one is above the law.

Governor is passionate that fairness and equality should not only be a way of life, but rights to which everyone is entitled. His message has the potential to bring hope and understanding to the general public, to local, state, and government entities, and to educational institutions that serve the criminal justice system. Each page of his book provides an intense focus on how to promote equality by demanding accountability.

www.ingramcontent.com/pod-product-compliance
Lightning Source LLC
Chambersburg PA
CBHW071120280326
41935CB00010B/1066